GW00373162

# Cycle TOURS

## South Wales

Nick Cotton

First published in 2002 by
Philip's Ltd, a division of
Octopus Publishing Group Ltd
2-4 Heron Quays
London E14 4JP

First edition 2002
First impression 2002

Based on the original Ordnance Survey Cycle Tours series
first published by Philip's and Ordnance Survey®.

ISBN 0-540-08211-2

The route maps in this book are reproduced from
Ordnance Survey® Landranger® mapping.

Text and compilation copyright © Philip's Ltd 2002

This product includes mapping data licensed from Ordnance
Survey® with the permission of the Controller of Her Majesty's
Stationery Office. © Crown copyright 2002. All rights reserved.
Licence number 100011710

**Photographic acknowledgements**

AA Photo Library 13, 28 • Nick Cotton 73, 85, 89, 93, 105, 117
• Colin Molyneux Associates 7, 19, 49, 52, 55, 61, 67, 80, 98,
101, 113 • Judy Todd 41

# Contents

# Abbreviations and symbols

## Directions

| | |
|---|---|
| L | left |
| R | right |
| LH | left-hand |
| RH | right-hand |
| SA | straight ahead or straight across |
| T-j | T-junction, a junction where you have to give way |
| X-roads | crossroads, a junction where you may or may not have to give way |
| 'Placename 2' | words in quotation marks are those that appear on signposts; the numbers indicate distance in miles unless stated otherwise |

## Distance and grade

The number of drink bottles indicates the grade:

- Easy
- Moderate
- Strenuous

The grade is based on the amount of climbing involved.

## Refreshments

Pubs and teashops on or near the route are listed. The tankard ♦ symbols indicate pubs particularly liked by the author.

# Page diagrams

The page diagrams on the introductory pages show how the map pages have been laid out, how they overlap and if any inset maps have been used.

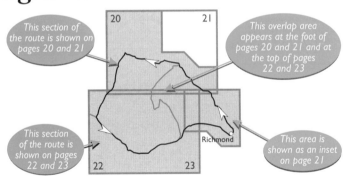

This section of the route is shown on pages 20 and 21

This overlap area appears at the foot of pages 20 and 21 and at the top of pages 22 and 23

This section of the route is shown on pages 22 and 23

This area is shown as an inset on page 21

Richmond

20  21  22  23

# Cross-profiles

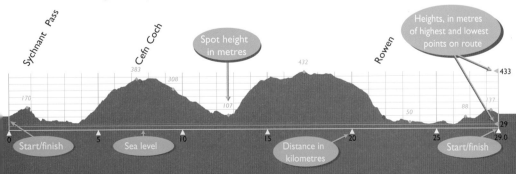

Sychnant Pass

Cefn Coch

Spot height in metres

Rowen

Heights, in metres of highest and lowest points on route

383  308  432  433  170  107  50  88  137  29

Start/finish  Sea level  Distance in kilometres  Start/finish

0  5  10  15  20  25  29.0

# Legend to 1:50 000 maps

## Roads and paths

**Motorway**

Service area (S)  M 5   Elevated

Junction number 20

**Motorway under construction**

**Trunk road**

Unfenced   Footbridge

A 46 (T)

**Main road**

Dual carriageway

A 420

**Main road under construction**

**Secondary road**

B 4348

**Narrow road with passing places**

A 855   B 885

**Road generally more than 4 m wide**

Bridge

**Road generally less than 4 m wide**

**Other road, drive or track**

**Path**

**Gradient: 1 in 5 and steeper, 1 in 7 to 1 in 5**

Gates   Road tunnel

Passenger ferry   Vehicle ferry

Ferry P   Ferry V

## Public rights of way (Not applicable to Scotland)

.................... Footpath

———————— Bridleway

—·—·—·—·— Road used as a public path

-+-+-+-+-+- Byway open to all traffic

Danger Area — Firing and test ranges in the area. Danger! Observe warning notices

## Tourist information

| | | |
|---|---|---|
| 🛈 | ℹ | Information centre, all year / seasonal |
| P | | Parking |
| ✕ | | Picnic site |
| ☼ | | Viewpoint |
| 人 | | Camp site |
| ⬛ | | Caravan site |
| ▲ | | Youth hostel |
| | | Selected places of tourist interest |
| ☎ | | Public telephone |
| ☎ | | Motoring organisation telephone |
| ⌐ | | Golf course or link |
| PC | | Public convenience (in rural areas) |

## Railways

Track: multiple or single

Track: narrow gauge

Bridges, footpath

Tunnel

Viaduct

Freight line, siding or tramway

Station, (a) principal, (b) closed to passengers

Level crossing  LC

Embankment

Cutting

## Rock features

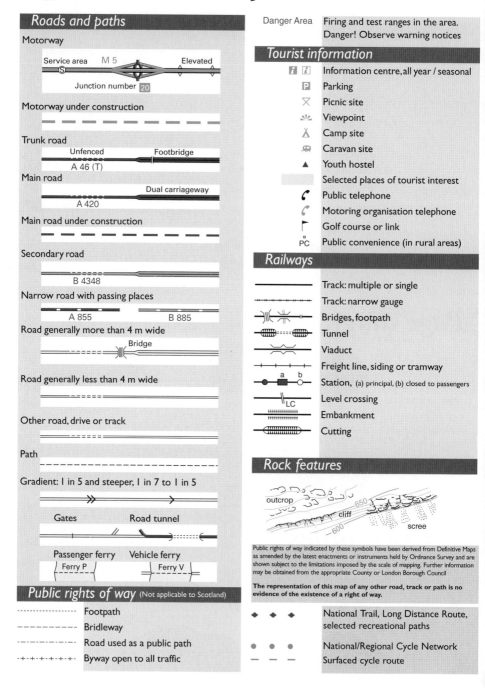

outcrop   cliff   scree   650   600

Public rights of way indicated by these symbols have been derived from Definitive Maps as amended by the latest enactments or instruments held by Ordnance Survey and are shown subject to the limitations imposed by the scale of mapping. Further information may be obtained from the appropriate County or London Borough Council

**The representation of this map of any other road, track or path is no evidence of the existence of a right of way.**

◆ ◆ ◆ National Trail, Long Distance Route, selected recreational paths

● ● ● National/Regional Cycle Network

— — — Surfaced cycle route

## Water features

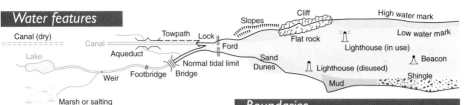

Canal (dry)
Canal
Lake
Weir  Footbridge  Bridge
Aqueduct
Towpath  Lock
Ford
Normal tidal limit
Marsh or salting

Slopes
Cliff
Flat rock
Sand
Dunes
Mud
High water mark
Low water mark
Lighthouse (in use)
Lighthouse (disused)
Beacon
Shingle

## General features

|  |  |
|---|---|
| ʌ——ʌ——ʌ | Electricity transmission line (with pylons spaced conventionally) |
| > - -> - -> | Pipeline (arrow indicates direction of flow) |
| ruin | Buildings |
|  | Public buildings (selected) |
|  | Bus or coach station |
|  | Coniferous wood |
|  | Non-coniferous wood |
|  | Mixed wood |
|  | Orchard |
|  | Park or ornamental grounds |
|  | Quarry |
|  | Spoil heap, refuse tip or dump |
| Ⴕ | Radio or TV mast |
| ♦ | Church or chapel with tower |
| ♦ | Church or chapel with spire |
| + | Church or chapel without tower or spire |
| ○ | Chimney or tower |
| ⌀ | Glasshouse |
| + | Graticule intersection at 5' intervals |
| Ⓗ | Heliport |
| △ | Triangulation pillar |
| Ⴟ | Windmill with or without sails |
| Ⴕ | Windpump |

## Boundaries

|  |  |
|---|---|
| + — + — + | National |
| –•–•–•–•–• | London borough |
|  | National park or forest park |
| NT | National Trust — NT open access / NT limited access |
| —•—•—•— | County, region or islands area |
| + + + + + | District |

## Abbreviations

|  |  |
|---|---|
| P | Post office |
| PH | Public house |
| MS | Milestone |
| MP | Milepost |
| CH | Clubhouse |
| PC | Public convenience (in rural areas) |
| TH | Town hall, guildhall or equivalent |
| CG | Coastguard |

## Antiquities

|  |  |
|---|---|
| VILLA | Roman |
| Castle | Non-Roman |
| ⤬ | Battlefield (with date) |
| ☆ | Tumulus |
| + | Position of antiquity which cannot be drawn to scale |
| ℳ | Ancient monuments and historic buildings in the care of the Secretaries of State for the Environment, for Scotland and for Wales and that are open to the public |

## Heights

|  |  |
|---|---|
| —50— | Contours are at 10 metres vertical interval |
| ·144 | Heights are to the nearest metre above mean sea level |

Heights shown close to a triangulation pillar refer to the station height at ground level and not necessarily to the summit

# In and out of the Ystwyth and Rheidol valleys east of Aberystwyth

There are no easy, quiet escape routes out of Aberystwyth by bike, so be prepared for traffic at the start and finish of this otherwise beautiful and challenging ride. The route heads south along the coast where the trees are blown sideways giving an indication of the prevailing wind's direction and strength. There is a climb of up to almost 240 m (800 ft) with spectacular views towards the Cambrian range of mountains before dropping down into the Ystwyth Valley. A second climb takes you up and over hills separating the two rivers, revealing more amazing views, and down to Devil's Bridge. There is a charge to see the falls, which is worth paying as they are most impressive, particularly after heavy rains. A short climb follows to the highest point of the ride before dropping down to the wooded valley of the Rheidol with an option to explore further upstream. The river is then followed all the way back to the start.

## Start

The railway station, Aberystwyth

P At the back of the railway station

## Distance and grade

54 km (34 miles), plus optional 10-km (6-mile) detour up the Rheidol Valley

Moderate/strenuous

## Terrain

Three main climbs – 170 m (560 ft) climb from the start to the radio mast near the coast, 120 m (380 ft) east from Llangwyryfon, 240 m (800 ft) from crossing the River Ystwyth near

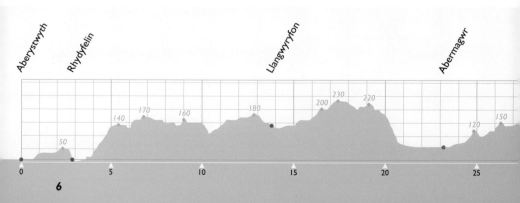

Abermagwr to the small reservoir of Llyn Ffongoch. Lowest point – sea level in Aberystwyth. Highest point – 310 m (1005 ft) at Mynydd Bach, west of Devil's Bridge

### Nearest railway
Aberystwyth

## Places of interest

### Devil's Bridge 14
The River Mynach cascades 91 m (300 ft) into a dark ravine, christened 'the dread chasm' by William Wordsworth. The village is remarkable for its three bridges, piled one on top of the other, across the Mynach Gorge. The earliest (medieval) bridge is known as 'The Bridge of the Evil One'; the 1753 bridge was built for horse-drawn traffic and the road bridge dates back to 1901

### Rheidol Power Station 19
The nerve centre of the hydroelectric power scheme, harnessing the water of Nant-y-moch and Dinas rivers. There are guided tours

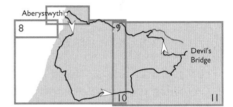

▲ Devil's Bridge

## Refreshments

The Mill PH 🍷, *plenty of choice in* **Aberystwyth**
*Hafod Arms PH, tearooms,* **Devil's Bridge**
*Halfway Inn* 🍷🍷*,* **Pisgah** *(just off the route)*
*Teas and coffees at Rheidol Hydro Project (seasonal)*
*Tynllidiart Arms PH* 🍷*,* **Capel Bangor**

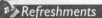

Devil's Bridge (Pontarfynach)    Aberffrwd    Capel Bangor    Llanbadarn Fawr

290  310    310  300

30    35    40    45    50    55

50    30    20    310  10

# ABERYSTWYTH

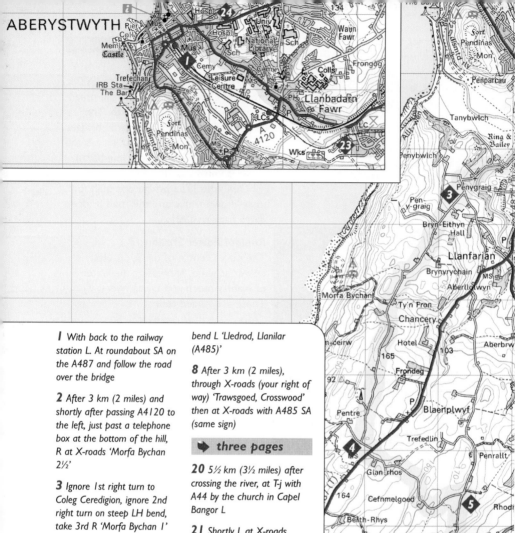

**1** With back to the railway station L. At roundabout SA on the A487 and follow the road over the bridge

**2** After 3 km (2 miles) and shortly after passing A4120 to the left, just past a telephone box at the bottom of the hill, R at X-roads 'Morfa Bychan 2½'

**3** Ignore 1st right turn to Coleg Ceredigion, ignore 2nd right turn on steep LH bend, take 3rd R 'Morfa Bychan 1'

**4** Pass trees blown horizontal by the wind and radio mast. At T-j with main road (A487) R then L (NS)

**5** Steep climb. At T-j R sharply back on yourself (NS)

**6** At T-j on hill bear L uphill, then shortly, at next T-j (with B4576) R 'Llangwyryfon, Llanilar'

**7** At bottom of the hill in Llangwyryfon on sharp RH

bend L 'Lledrod, Llanilar (A485)'

**8** After 3 km (2 miles), through X-roads (your right of way) 'Trawsgoed, Crosswood' then at X-roads with A485 SA (same sign)

### ➡ three pages

**20** 5½ km (3½ miles) after crossing the river, at T-j with A44 by the church in Capel Bangor L

**21** Shortly L at X-roads beyond Post Office (NS). Cross bridge and railway and follow signs for Llanbadarn Fawr

**22** At T-j by trading estate bear R. The return to the start is unavoidably on main roads

**23** At T-j with A44 L

**24** After 3 km (2 miles) at T-j with A487 at Penglais Terrace L and follow the one-way system back to the start at the railway station

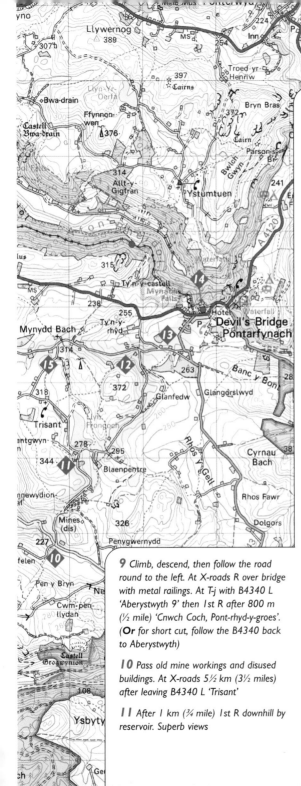

**12** At T-j R sharply back on yourself for Devil's Bridge (waterfalls, pub, tea shops) (**Or** left for continuation of route, missing out Devil's Bridge)

**13** At T-j (with school to the right) L on B4343 'Devil's Bridge', then at the T-j with A4120 R to visit waterfalls

**14** (Retrace route). With back to the Hafod Arms PH L towards Aberystwyth, then 1st L by memorial cross onto the B4343 'Pont-rhyd-y-groes, Tregaron'. After 600 m (yd), just before school, 1st R 'Mynydd Bach'

**15** After 2 km (1¼ miles), immediately after the brow of the hill, on sharp LH bend next R past sycamore trees towards white house (NS)

**16** At T-j by house called Plynlimon View, with track ahead, R (NS). Shortly, follow road round to the R

**17** At T-j with main road (A4120) L 'Aberystwyth' then after 1 km (¾ mile) 1st R 'Aberffrwd' (**Or** stay on A4120 towards Aberystwyth for 3 km (2 miles) for excellent refreshment stop at the Halfway Inn)

**18** At T-j soon after crossing miniature railway R sharply back on yourself 'Capel Bangor'

**19** Cross bridge and at T-j L 'Aberystwyth, Capel Bangor' (**Or** turn R for detour up the valley – Rheidol Hydro Scheme, teas and coffees, some unusual wooden carvings and small waterfalls)

**20** 5 km (3½ miles) after crossing the river, at T-j with A44 by the church in Capel Bangor L

**21** Shortly L at X-roads beyond Post Office (NS). Cross bridge and railway and follow signs for Llanbadarn Fawr

◄ three pages

**9** Climb, descend, then follow the road round to the left. At X-roads R over bridge with metal railings. At T-j with B4340 L 'Aberystwyth 9' then 1st R after 800 m (½ mile) 'Cnwch Coch, Pont-rhyd-y-groes'. (**Or** for short cut, follow the B4340 back to Aberystwyth)

**10** Pass old mine workings and disused buildings. At X-roads 5½ km (3½ miles) after leaving B4340 L 'Trisant'

**11** After 1 km (¾ mile) 1st R downhill by reservoir. Superb views

# 2 *From Rhayader to Llanidloes returning via the Wye Valley*

**Start**

The clocktower, Rhayader

P Follow signs

**Distance and grade**

54 km (34 miles)

///// Strenuous
(But a there-and-back ride from Rhayader to Llangurig along the beautiful, flat Wye Valley would be very easy)

**Terrain**

Three major climbs and several shorter ones – 210 m (700 ft) eastwards from Rhayader with one particularly steep section; 120 m (410 ft) from Abbeycwmhir to

**R**hayader is a fine little town in the heart of Wales and a good base for bike tours both on- and off-road. The ride climbs eastwards to almost 430 m (1400 ft) – with one particularly steep section – before dropping down to Abbeycwmhir. As might be expected, there are superb views back to the west. Another very different feature soon dominates the horizons – the ranks of wind turbines set high on the hills for maximum effect to capture the wind's energy. The dilemma is there in a nutshell: does the generation of environmentally friendly energy justify the intrusion of metal wind turbines in an area of outstanding beauty? After cycling for many kilometres in the hills, the descent into Llanidloes offers a chance of a variety of refreshments. The last major climb takes you out of the valley of the River Dulas and down into the Wye Valley that is followed, along a delightful road, all the way back to Rhayader.

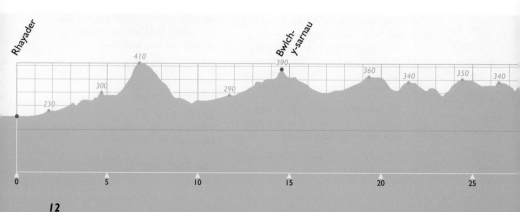

Bwlch-y-Sarnau; 170 m (560 ft) between Llanidloes and Llangurig. Lowest point – 170 m (560 ft) at Llanidloes. Highest point – 420 m (1380 ft) between Rhayader and Abbeycwmhir

 Nearest railway

Crossgates, 13 km (8 miles) east of Rhayader or Caersws, 13 km (8 miles) north-east of Llanidloes

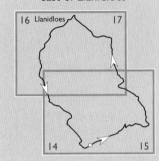

 Places of interest

### Rhayader 1
Sheltered on all sides by mountains, this small market town is itself 210 m (700 ft) above sea level and lies on the River Wye. It is also the gateway to the Elan Valley – the Welsh 'Lake District' – and the man-made dams and reservoirs to the west are impressive

### Abbey Cwmhir 4
Ruined, Cistercian 'Abbey in the Long Valley' lies below hills of 460 m (1500 ft)

▲ The River Wye near Rhayader

 Refreshments

Bear PH 🍺, Castle PH 🍺, plenty of choice in **Rhayader**
Happy Union PH, **Abbeycwmhir**
Plenty of choice in **Llanidloes**
Blue Bell PH, **Llangurig**

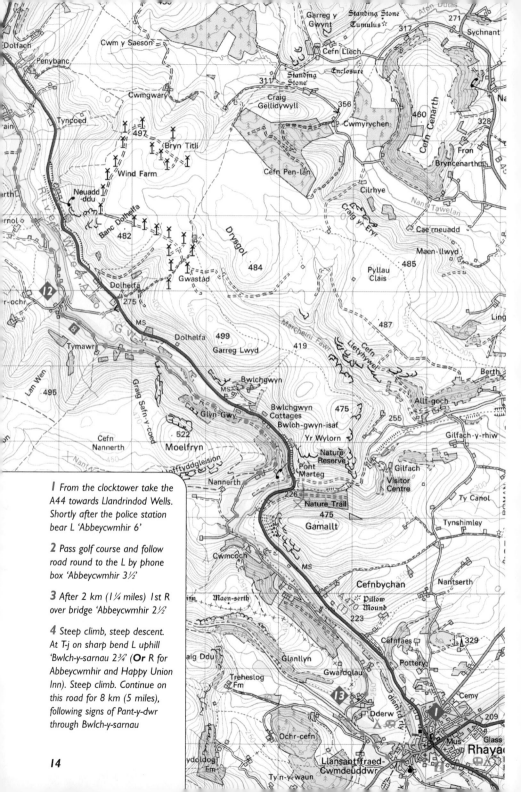

**1** From the clocktower take the A44 towards Llandrindod Wells. Shortly after the police station bear L 'Abbeycwmhir 6'

**2** Pass golf course and follow road round to the L by phone box 'Abbeycwmhir 3½'

**3** After 2 km (1¼ miles) 1st R over bridge 'Abbeycwmhir 2½'

**4** Steep climb, steep descent. At T-j on sharp bend L uphill 'Bwlch-y-sarnau 2¾' (**Or** R for Abbeycwmhir and Happy Union Inn). Steep climb. Continue on this road for 8 km (5 miles), following signs of Pant-y-dwr through Bwlch-y-sarnau

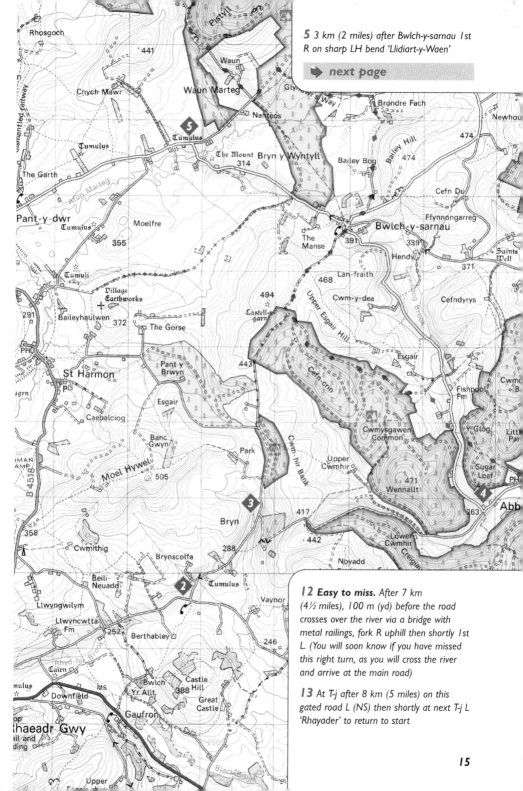

**5** 3 km (2 miles) after Bwlch-y-sarnau 1st R on sharp LH bend 'Llidiart-y-Waen'

➡ *next page*

**12 Easy to miss.** After 7 km (4½ miles), 100 m (yd) before the road crosses over the river via a bridge with metal railings, fork R uphill then shortly 1st L. (You will soon know if you have missed this right turn, as you will cross the river and arrive at the main road)

**13** At T-j after 8 km (5 miles) on this gated road L (NS) then shortly at next T-j L 'Rhayader' to return to start

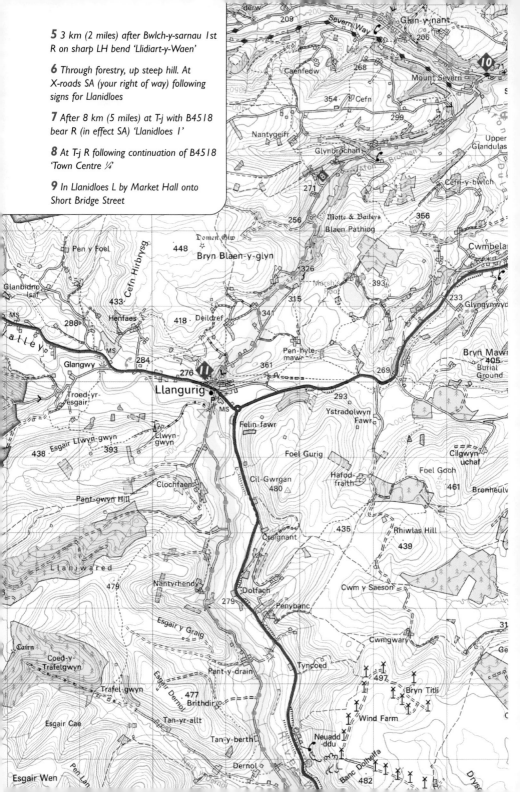

**5** 3 km (2 miles) after Bwlch-y-sarnau 1st R on sharp LH bend 'Llidiart-y-Waen'

**6** Through forestry, up steep hill. At X-roads SA (your right of way) following signs for Llanidloes

**7** After 8 km (5 miles) at T-j with B4518 bear R (in effect SA) 'Llanidloes 1'

**8** At T-j R following continuation of B4518 'Town Centre ¼'

**9** In Llanidloes L by Market Hall onto Short Bridge Street

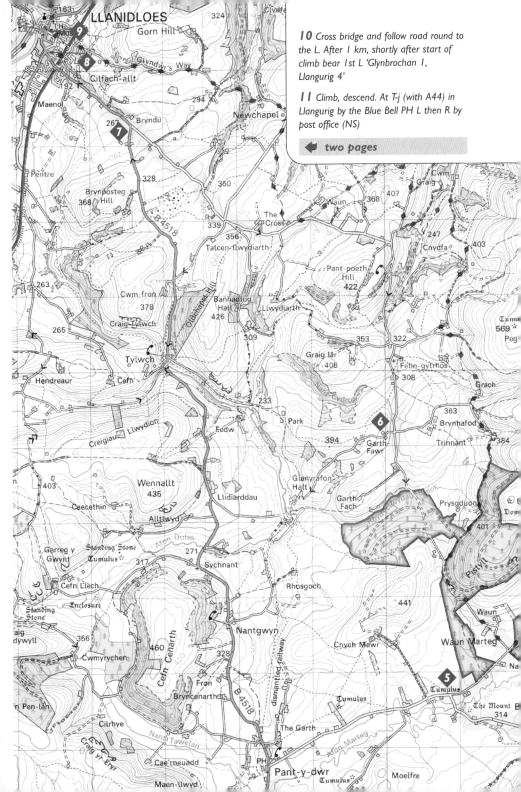

**10** *Cross bridge and follow road round to the L. After 1 km, shortly after start of climb bear 1st L 'Glynbrochan 1, Llangurig 4'*

**11** *Climb, descend. At T-j (with A44) in Llangurig by the Blue Bell PH L then R by post office (NS)*

◀ two pages

# 3 The Devil's Staircase and the Llyn Brianne Reservoir west of Llanwrtyd Wells

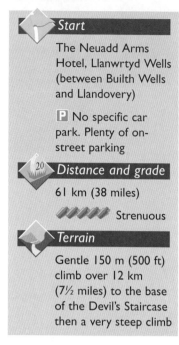

**Start**

The Neuadd Arms Hotel, Llanwrtyd Wells (between Builth Wells and Llandovery)

**P** No specific car park. Plenty of on-street parking

**Distance and grade**

61 km (38 miles)

Strenuous

**Terrain**

Gentle 150 m (500 ft) climb over 12 km (7½ miles) to the base of the Devil's Staircase then a very steep climb

**A** beautiful ride in the heart of sparsely populated Mid-Wales with many highlights. The ride starts gently with a long, steady climb to the north up a valley formed by the River Irfon. Nothing prepares you for the almost vertical ascent of the Devil's Staircase. Only extreme enthusiasts should try to cycle up it. Together with a climb up from the Wye Valley on the Builth Route and a hill south of Monmouth, the Devil's Staircase represents a very tough road climb. A fast and furious descent drops you down into the Tywi Valley. The Tywi fills the spectacular Llyn Brianne Reservoir, which is followed for several kilometres. Another fast descent takes you past two of the few refreshment stops on the ride – the Towy Bridge Inn and the Royal Oak at Rhandirmwyn. Magnificent views to the north follow the steep climb up from Rhandirmwyn. The descent will test your brakes to the maximum. The final climb to Tirabad avoids the traffic on the A483.

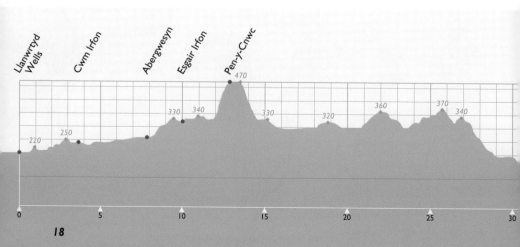

– a further 120 m (400 ft). Several short climbs around the reservoir. 150 m (500 ft) climb south from Towy Bridge through Rhandirmwyn. 190 m (620 ft) between Cynghordy and Tirabad. Lowest point – 120 m (390 ft) at Towy Bridge PH. Highest point – 480 m (1570 ft) at the top of the Devil's Staircase

## Nearest railway

Llanwrtyd Wells

▶ Llyn Brianne reservoir

## Places of interest

### Llanwrtyd Wells 1
The tranquillity of the place belies those bygone days when 'taking the waters' was fashionable and this spa town was bursting at the seams with holidaymakers from the industrial areas of South Wales

### Abergwesyn Pass 3
Narrow pass between Abergwesyn and Tregaron called the Devil's Staircase. Steep hairpin bends rise and fall in roller-coaster style through wild moorland with panoramic views

## Refreshments

*Plenty of choice in* **Llanwrtyd Wells**
*Towy Bridge PH, north of* **Rhandirmwyn**
*Royal Oak PH,* **Rhandirmwyn**
*Glanbran Arms PH,* **Cynghordy**

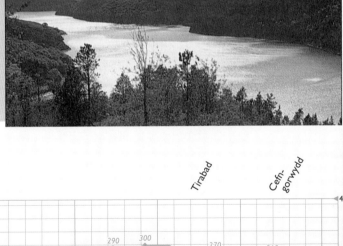

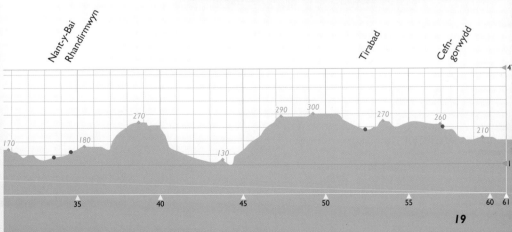

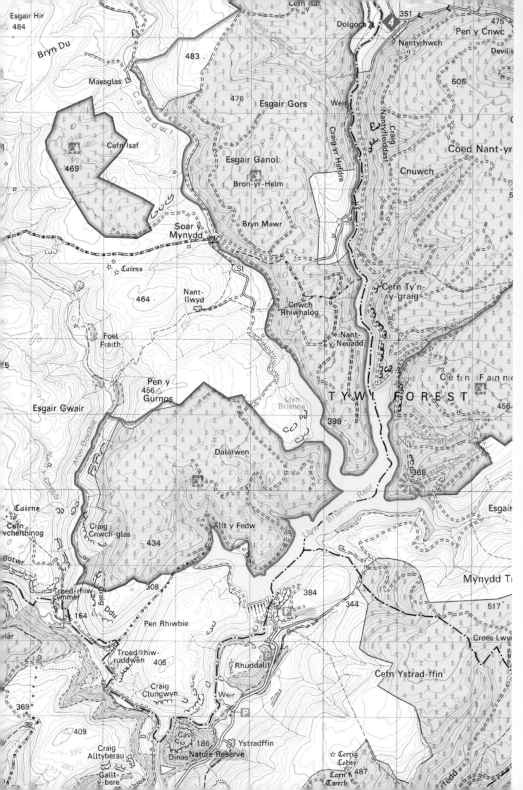

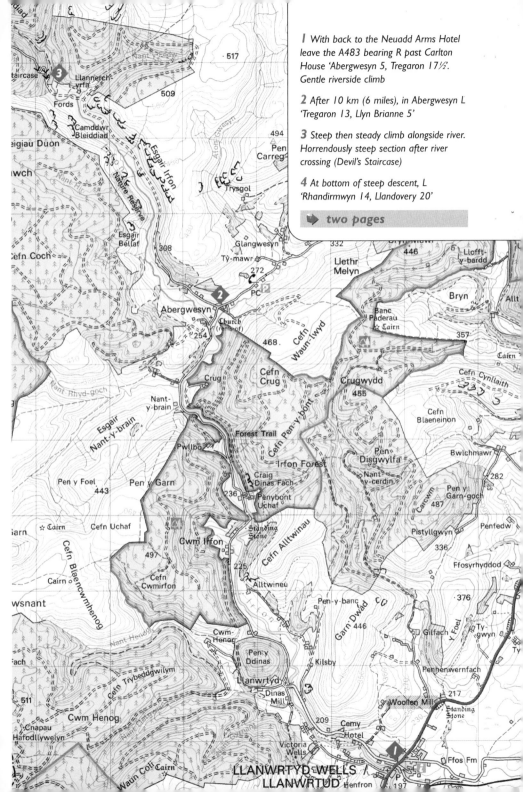

1 With back to the Neuadd Arms Hotel leave the A483 bearing R past Carlton House 'Abergwesyn 5, Tregaron 17½'. Gentle riverside climb

2 After 10 km (6 miles), in Abergwesyn L 'Tregaron 13, Llyn Brianne 5'

3 Steep then steady climb alongside river. Horrendously steep section after river crossing (Devil's Staircase)

4 At bottom of steep descent, L 'Rhandirmwyn 14, Llandovery 20'

➡ two pages

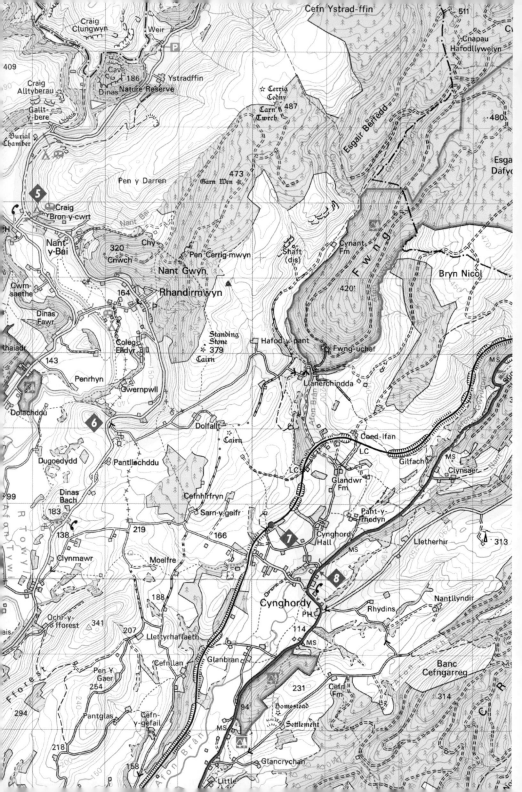

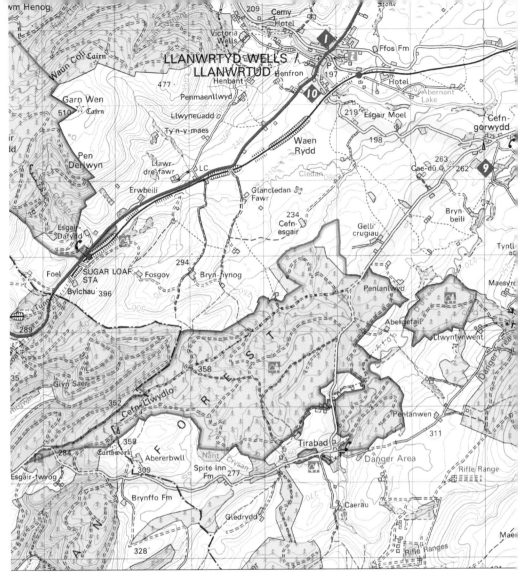

**5** After 19 km (12 miles), having dropped to the valley bottom after contouring the reservoir, SA following signs for Rhandirmwyn

**6 Easy to miss.** 3 km (2 miles) after passing the Royal Oak PH in Rhandirmwyn 1st L 'Youth Hostel 1½'. Steep climb, fine views. Very steep descent. Go beneath viaduct

**7** 1 km (¾ mile) after recrossing stream 1st L '6 ft 6 in width limit'

**8** At T-j (with A483) R into Cynghordy, then after 1 km (¾ mile), shortly after church 1st L 'Tirabad 5'. Gentle climb to Tirabad over 8 km (5 miles). Lovely ridge section

**9 Easy to miss.** 5½ km (3½ miles) after Tirabad and shortly after passing mast 1st L 'Llanwrtyd Wells 2'

**10** At T-j with A483 R to return to start

# 4 ◢ Linking the river valleys north and west of Llandovery

Llandovery is one of several small, attractive towns in Mid-Wales that serve as good bases for cycling tours and this ride is relatively easy for the area. There are two gentle climbs, the first of which follows the scenic valley of the River Tywi for some 13 km (8 miles). Outlying sheep farms surrounded by well-maintained hedgerows alternate with forestry plantations along the route. The road through Talley is busier than would normally be chosen but it has the advantages of taking you past a good pub at Talley, the ruins of the abbey in the same village and, not least, it avoids a 210 m (700 ft) climb. The second ascent of the ride starts east of Llangadog and climbs through woodland before a fast descent back into the Tywi Valley near to Llandovery.

## Start

The Kings Head PH in the centre of Llandovery

P Follow signs

## Distance and grade

56 km (35 miles)

◢◢◢ Moderate

## Terrain

Gentle climb over 200 m (650 ft) from the start, through two valleys, to the highpoint of the ride. Second climb of 110 m (350 ft) east of Llangadog, starting gently then becoming steeper. Lowest point – 46 m (150 ft) at crossing of River Tywi near to Llangadog. Highest point – 260 m (850 ft) at the pass between the Tywi and the Cothi valleys (instruction 6)

## Nearest railway

Llandovery

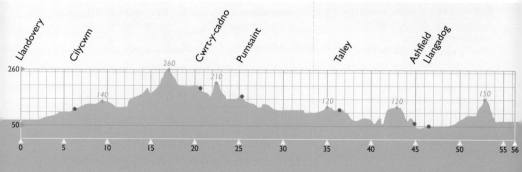

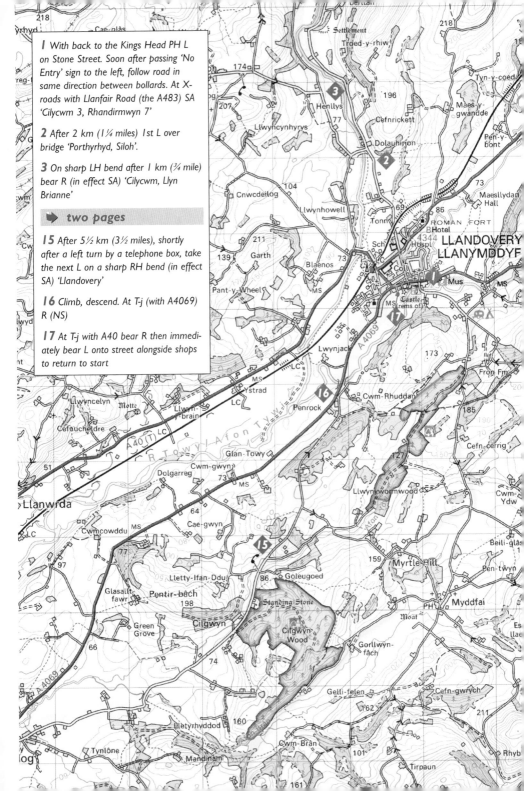

**1** With back to the Kings Head PH L on Stone Street. Soon after passing 'No Entry' sign to the left, follow road in same direction between bollards. At X-roads with Llanfair Road (the A483) SA 'Cilycwm 3, Rhandirmwyn 7'

**2** After 2 km (1¼ miles) 1st L over bridge 'Porthyrhyd, Siloh'.

**3** On sharp LH bend after 1 km (¾ mile) bear R (in effect SA) 'Cilycwm, Llyn Brianne'

➡ **two pages**

**15** After 5½ km (3½ miles), shortly after a left turn by a telephone box, take the next L on a sharp RH bend (in effect SA) 'Llandovery'

**16** Climb, descend. At T-j (with A4069) R (NS)

**17** At T-j with A40 bear R then immediately bear L onto street alongside shops to return to start

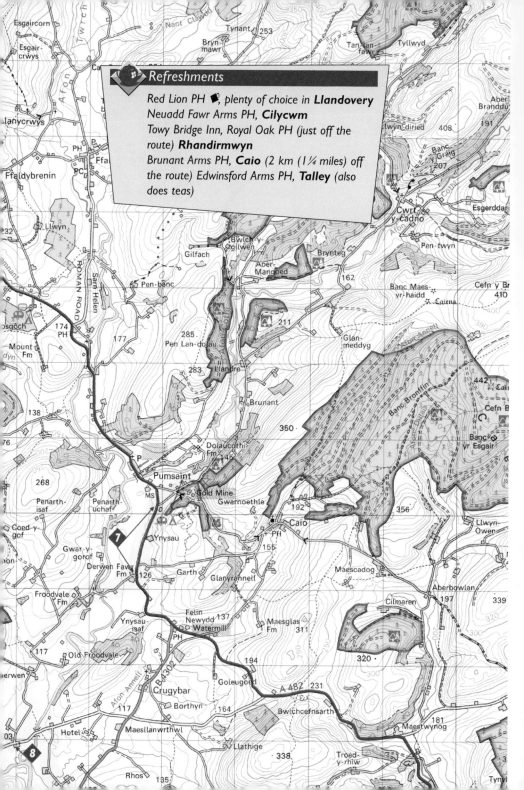

## Refreshments

Red Lion PH 🍺, plenty of choice in **Llandovery**
Neuadd Fawr Arms PH, **Cilycwm**
Towy Bridge Inn, Royal Oak PH (just off the route) **Rhandirmwyn**
Brunant Arms PH, **Caio** (2 km (1¼ miles) off the route) Edwinsford Arms PH, **Talley** (also does teas)

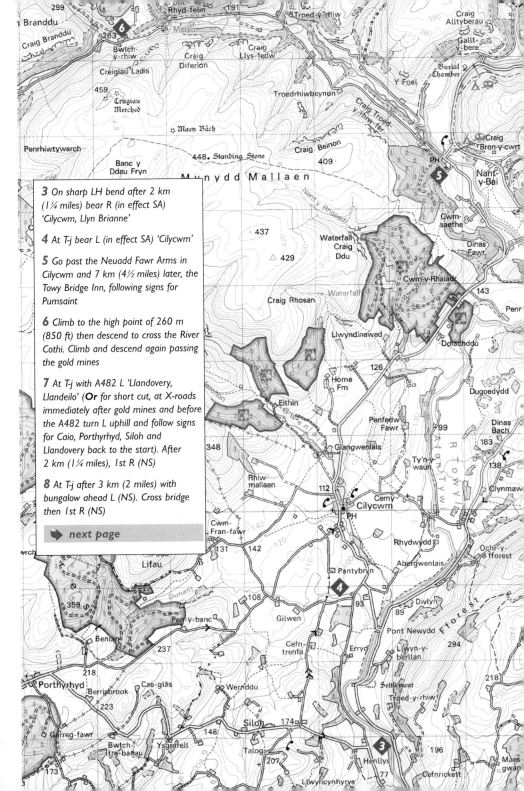

**3** On sharp LH bend after 2 km (1¼ miles) bear R (in effect SA) 'Cilycwm, Llyn Brianne'

**4** At T-j bear L (in effect SA) 'Cilycwm'

**5** Go past the Neuadd Fawr Arms in Cilycwm and 7 km (4½ miles) later, the Towy Bridge Inn, following signs for Pumsaint

**6** Climb to the high point of 260 m (850 ft) then descend to cross the River Cothi. Climb and descend again passing the gold mines

**7** At T-j with A482 L 'Llandovery, Llandeilo' (**Or** for short cut, at X-roads immediately after gold mines and before the A482 turn L uphill and follow signs for Caio, Porthyrhyd, Siloh and Llandovery back to the start). After 2 km (1¼ miles), 1st R (NS)

**8** At T-j after 3 km (2 miles) with bungalow ahead L (NS). Cross bridge then 1st R (NS)

➡ **next page**

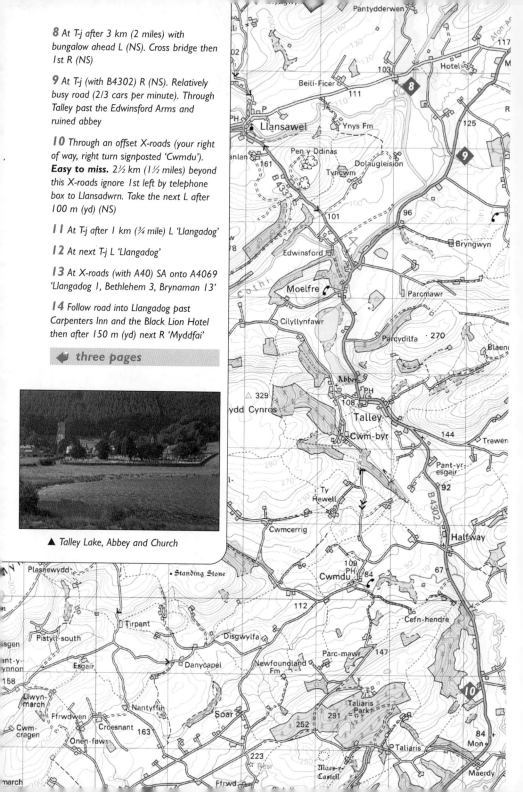

**8** At T-j after 3 km (2 miles) with bungalow ahead L (NS). Cross bridge then 1st R (NS)

**9** At T-j (with B4302) R (NS). Relatively busy road (2/3 cars per minute). Through Talley past the Edwinsford Arms and ruined abbey

**10** Through an offset X-roads (your right of way, right turn signposted 'Cwmdu'). **Easy to miss.** 2½ km (1½ miles) beyond this X-roads ignore 1st left by telephone box to Llansadwrn. Take the next L after 100 m (yd) (NS)

**11** At T-j after 1 km (¾ mile) L 'Llangadog'

**12** At next T-j L 'Llangadog'

**13** At X-roads (with A40) SA onto A4069 'Llangadog 1, Bethlehem 3, Brynaman 13'

**14** Follow road into Llangadog past Carpenters Inn and the Black Lion Hotel then after 150 m (yd) next R 'Myddfai'

▶ **three pages**

▲ Talley Lake, Abbey and Church

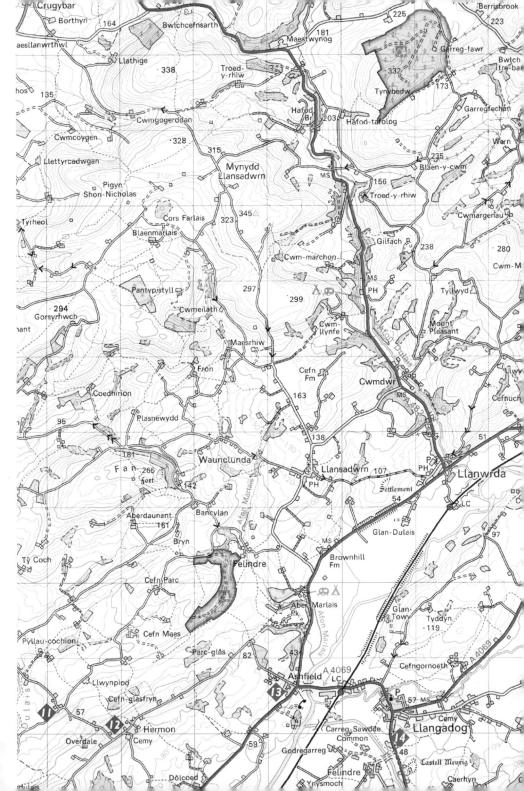

# 5 *From Builth Wells to Brecon over Mynydd Eppynt returning via the Wye Valley*

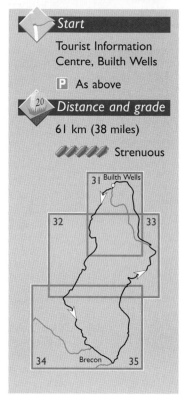

Start

Tourist Information Centre, Builth Wells

P  As above

Distance and grade

61 km (38 miles)

Strenuous

**M**uch of the upland area of Mynydd Eppynt is used by the army, and roads to the west can be shut on certain days. This ride stays on the east side of the hills, out of Builth Wells and through a delightful valley formed by the River Duhonw. Green slopes and woodland give way to moorland as the ride climbs to a high point of almost 430 m (1400 ft) near the Griffin Inn. The descent takes you down the green and wooded valley of the Ysgir and into Brecon, a busy market town serving a wide catchment area of the Brecon Beacons and Black Mountains. The first of the two climbs back to Builth Wells runs over several kilometres through Llandew and into the forestry at Llaneglwys. The second rises almost vertically from the Wye Valley near Erwood on a narrow, roller coaster lane. A more gentle alternative is also given, which follows the valley on the B4567 to the east of the River Wye.

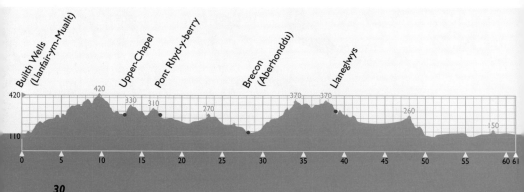

**30**

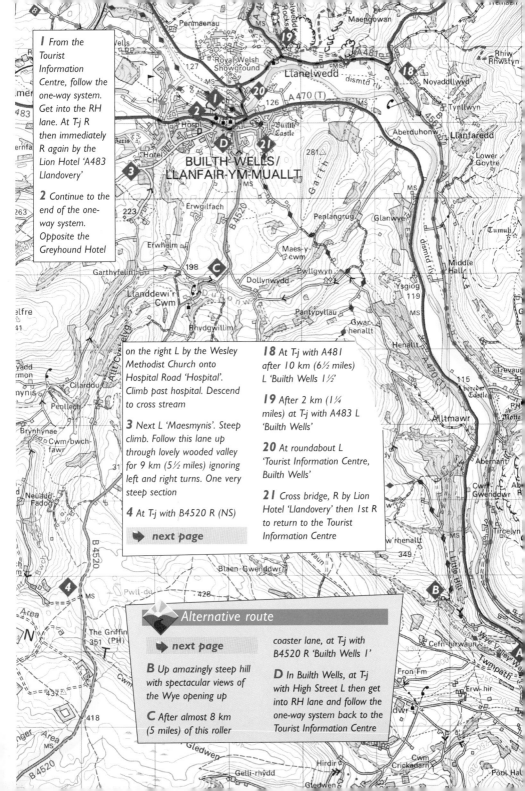

**1** From the Tourist Information Centre, follow the one-way system. Get into the RH lane. At T-j R then immediately R again by the Lion Hotel 'A483 Llandovery'

**2** Continue to the end of the one-way system. Opposite the Greyhound Hotel

on the right L by the Wesley Methodist Church onto Hospital Road 'Hospital'. Climb past hospital. Descend to cross stream

**3** Next L 'Maesmynis'. Steep climb. Follow this lane up through lovely wooded valley for 9 km (5½ miles) ignoring left and right turns. One very steep section

**4** At T-j with B4520 R (NS)

➡ next page

**18** At T-j with A481 after 10 km (6½ miles) L 'Builth Wells 1½'

**19** After 2 km (1¼ miles) at T-j with A483 L 'Builth Wells'

**20** At roundabout L 'Tourist Information Centre, Builth Wells'

**21** Cross bridge, R by Lion Hotel 'Llandovery' then 1st R to return to the Tourist Information Centre

### Alternative route

➡ next page

**B** Up amazingly steep hill with spectacular views of the Wye opening up

**C** After almost 8 km (5 miles) of this roller coaster lane, at T-j with B4520 R 'Builth Wells 1'

**D** In Builth Wells, at T-j with High Street L then get into RH lane and follow the one-way system back to the Tourist Information Centre

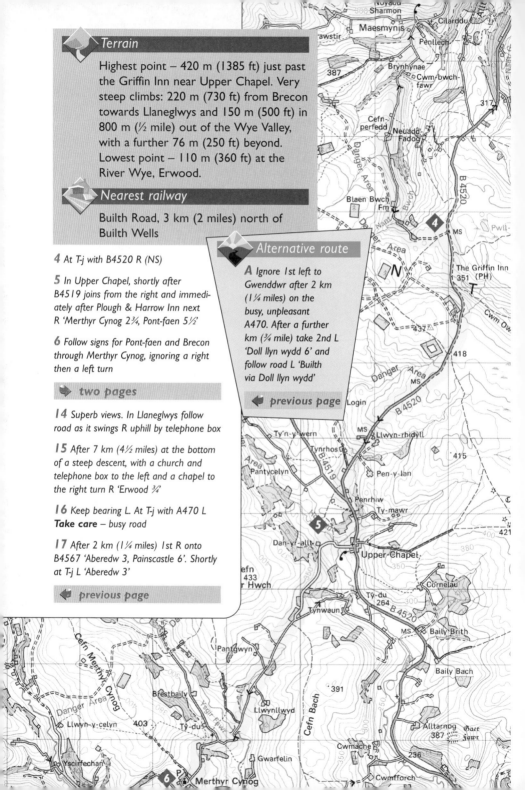

## Terrain

Highest point – 420 m (1385 ft) just past the Griffin Inn near Upper Chapel. Very steep climbs: 220 m (730 ft) from Brecon towards Llaneglwys and 150 m (500 ft) in 800 m (½ mile) out of the Wye Valley, with a further 76 m (250 ft) beyond. Lowest point – 110 m (360 ft) at the River Wye, Erwood.

## Nearest railway

Builth Road, 3 km (2 miles) north of Builth Wells

**4** At T-j with B4520 R (NS)

**5** In Upper Chapel, shortly after B4519 joins from the right and immediately after Plough & Harrow Inn next R 'Merthyr Cynog 2¾, Pont-faen 5½'

**6** Follow signs for Pont-faen and Brecon through Merthyr Cynog, ignoring a right then a left turn

➡ **two pages**

**14** Superb views. In Llaneglwys follow road as it swings R uphill by telephone box

**15** After 7 km (4½ miles) at the bottom of a steep descent, with a church and telephone box to the left and a chapel to the right turn R 'Erwood ¾'

**16** Keep bearing L. At T-j with A470 L **Take care** – busy road

**17** After 2 km (1¼ miles) 1st R onto B4567 'Aberedw 3, Painscastle 6'. Shortly at T-j L 'Aberedw 3'

⬅ **previous page**

## Alternative route

**A** Ignore 1st left to Gwenddwr after 2 km (1¼ miles) on the busy, unpleasant A470. After a further km (¾ mile) take 2nd L 'Doll llyn wydd 6' and follow road L 'Builth via Doll llyn wydd'

⬅ **previous page**

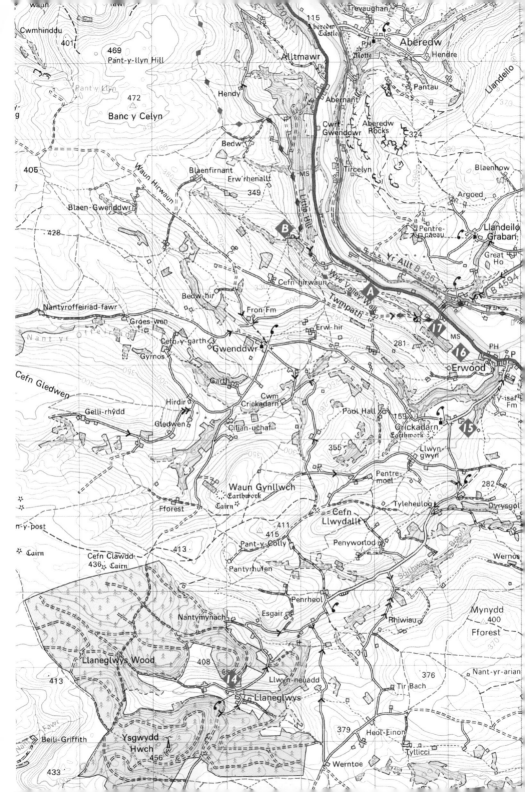

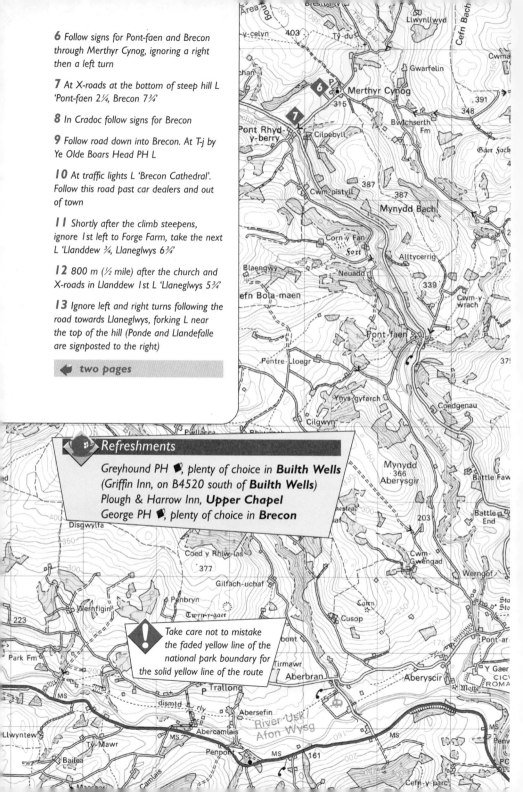

**6** Follow signs for Pont-faen and Brecon through Merthyr Cynog, ignoring a right then a left turn

**7** At X-roads at the bottom of steep hill L 'Pont-faen 2¼, Brecon 7¾'

**8** In Cradoc follow signs for Brecon

**9** Follow road down into Brecon. At T-j by Ye Olde Boars Head PH L

**10** At traffic lights L 'Brecon Cathedral'. Follow this road past car dealers and out of town

**11** Shortly after the climb steepens, ignore 1st left to Forge Farm, take the next L 'Llanddew ¾, Llaneglwys 6¾'

**12** 800 m (½ mile) after the church and X-roads in Llanddew 1st L 'Llaneglwys 5¾'

**13** Ignore left and right turns following the road towards Llaneglwys, forking L near the top of the hill (Ponde and Llandefalle are signposted to the right)

◀ two pages

## Refreshments

Greyhound PH 🍺, plenty of choice in **Builth Wells** (Griffin Inn, on B4520 south of **Builth Wells**)
Plough & Harrow Inn, **Upper Chapel**
George PH 🍺, plenty of choice in **Brecon**

⚠ Take care not to mistake the faded yellow line of the national park boundary for the solid yellow line of the route

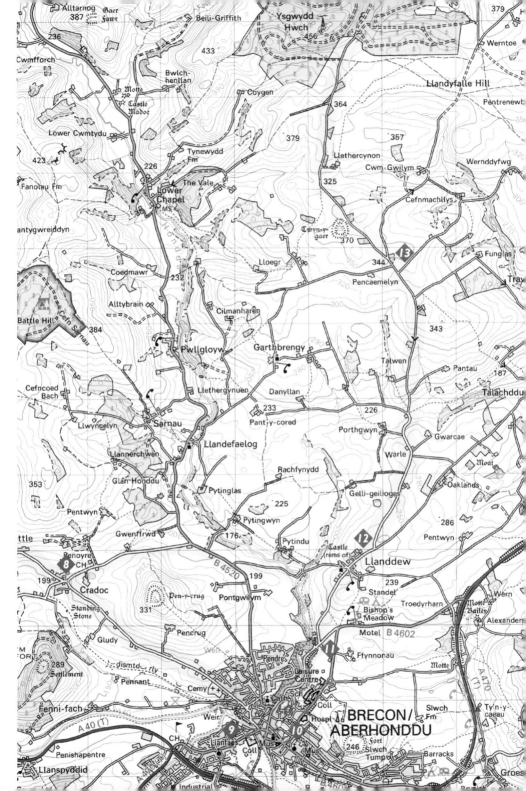

# 6 *West from Brecon with dramatic views of the Beacons*

**B**recon serves a wide area west of
Abergavenny and north of Merthyr Tydfil,
including much of the Brecon Beacons and
the Black Mountains; it is consequently
busier than other towns of a similar size.
For cyclists, however, there are several
escape routes on minor roads out into the
hills. The ride heads west past the old
Roman fort at Y Gaer before following the
Nant Bran Valley northwest towards
Llanfihangel Nant Bran. A further climb to
the south reveals the array of mountains
forming a backdrop to Sennybridge. For
those on mountain bikes, in the east of
Crai, there are alternatives to cycling 3 km
(2 miles) on the A4067 (although this is
not particularly busy for an A road). The
highpoint of the ride is reached soon after
leaving the main road. From here back to
Brecon, the views are spectacular, and a 6½ km (4 mile) descent to a
roundabout with the A40 on the outskirts of Brecon is one of the best in
the country with the glorious panorama of the Beacons stretching away
to the east.

## Start

Ye Olde Boars Head
PH, near the bridge
over the River Usk,
Brecon

P Car park just off
the road towards
Cradoc at the start of
the ride

## Distance and grade

48 km (30 miles)

Strenuous

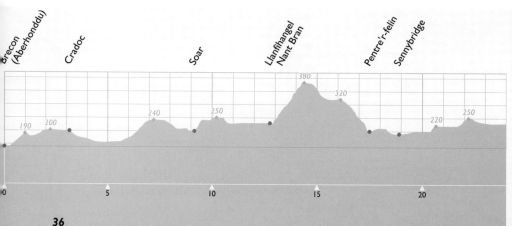

## Terrain

Between Brecon and Llanfihangel, there are three climbs of 76 m (250 ft); three other main climbs: 150 m (500 feet) southwest from Llanfihangel; 240 m (800 ft) from Sennybridge to the highpoint east of Crai; 100 m (330 ft) from the Senni river up onto Mynydd Illtud. Lowest point – 140 m (460 ft) in Brecon. Highest point – 420 m (1380 ft) south of Crai (instructions 10/11)

## Nearest railway

Llandovery, 19 km (12 miles) west of Sennybridge

## Refreshments

*George PH 🍺, plenty of choice in **Brecon***
*Shoemakers Arms PH 🍺, **Pentre-bach** (3 km (2 miles) north of the route at instruction 5)*
*Usk and Railway PH, teas and coffees in **Sennybridge***

## Places of interest

### Brecon 1

In the Zulu War of 1879, 141 men (36 of whom were hospital patients) fought off an attack by 4000 Zulus at Rorke's Drift in South Africa. Their story, and that of the entire Zulu War, is told in the Zulu War Room of the 24th Regiment Museum, alongside exhibits and artefacts that include campaign medals, Zulu shields and weapons. The museum is within Brecon's army base

### Y Gaer 2 *(just off the route)*

The name means 'the fort': it was one of the strongholds of the Romans. Originally built of earth and timber in about AD 80, and then rebuilt in stone about 60 years later, it housed a garrison of 500 men

### Sarn Helen 11

When the Romans conquered Wales in AD 74, they pinned the country down with a system of fortresses and roads. One of these roads was Sarn Helen, which linked South Wales with the coast road running from Chester to Caernarfon

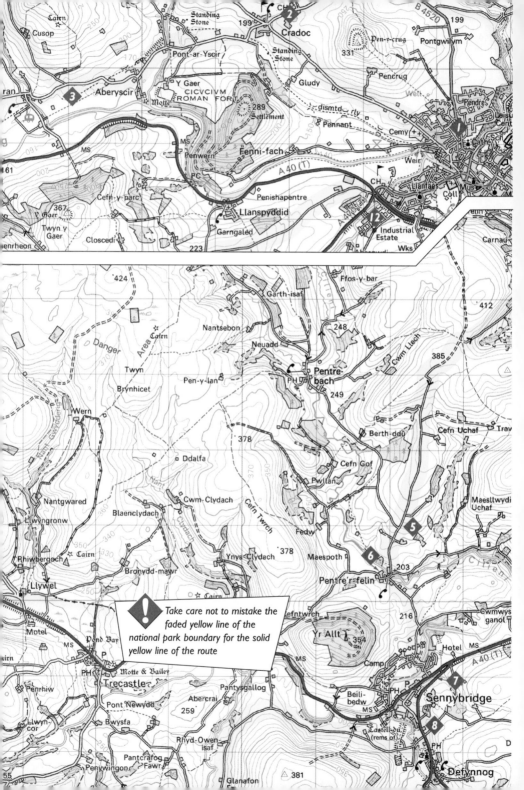

Take care not to mistake the faded yellow line of the national park boundary for the solid yellow line of the route

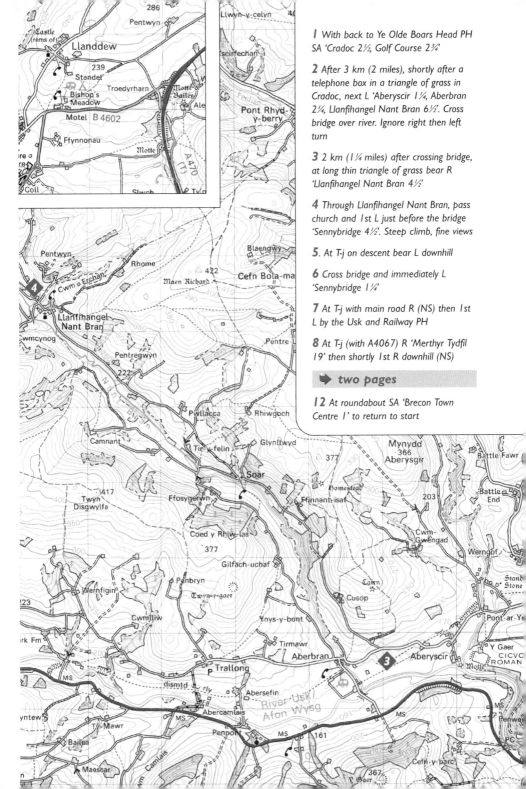

**1** With back to Ye Olde Boars Head PH SA 'Cradoc 2½, Golf Course 2¾'

**2** After 3 km (2 miles), shortly after a telephone box in a triangle of grass in Cradoc, next L 'Aberyscir 1¼, Aberbran 2¼, Llanfihangel Nant Bran 6½'. Cross bridge over river. Ignore right then left turn

**3** 2 km (1¼ miles) after crossing bridge, at long thin triangle of grass bear R 'Llanfihangel Nant Bran 4½'

**4** Through Llanfihangel Nant Bran, pass church and 1st L just before the bridge 'Sennybridge 4½'. Steep climb, fine views

**5**. At T-j on descent bear L downhill

**6** Cross bridge and immediately L 'Sennybridge 1¼'

**7** At T-j with main road R (NS) then 1st L by the Usk and Railway PH

**8** At T-j (with A4067) R 'Merthyr Tydfil 19' then shortly 1st R downhill (NS)

➡ **two pages**

**12** At roundabout SA 'Brecon Town Centre 1' to return to start

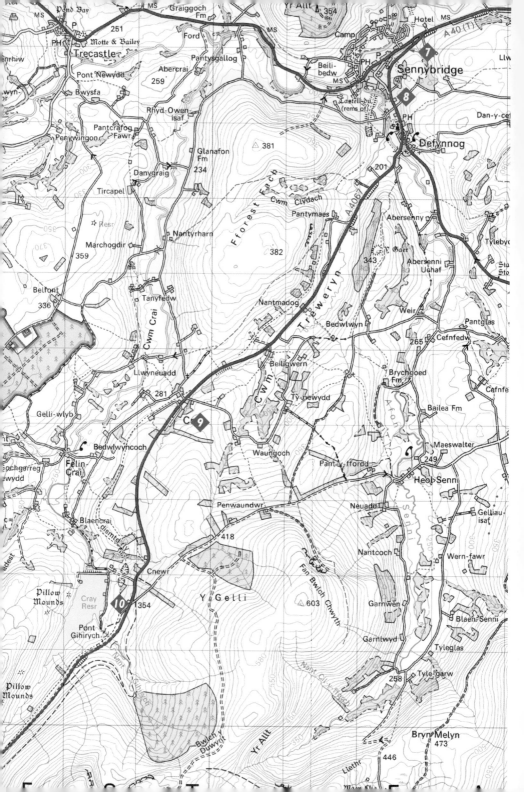

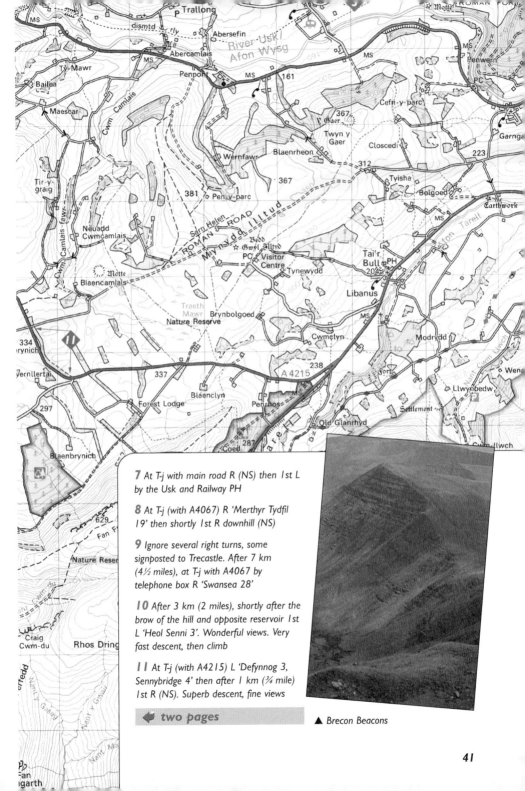

**7** At T-j with main road R (NS) then 1st L by the Usk and Railway PH

**8** At T-j (with A4067) R 'Merthyr Tydfil 19' then shortly 1st R downhill (NS)

**9** Ignore several right turns, some signposted to Trecastle. After 7 km (4½ miles), at T-j with A4067 by telephone box R 'Swansea 28'

**10** After 3 km (2 miles), shortly after the brow of the hill and opposite reservoir 1st L 'Heol Senni 3'. Wonderful views. Very fast descent, then climb

**11** At T-j (with A4215) L 'Defynnog 3, Sennybridge 4' then after 1 km (¾ mile) 1st R (NS). Superb descent, fine views

◀ **two pages**

▲ Brecon Beacons

# From the coast to Cardigan via a lovely wooded valley

**Start**

The clocktower and Library in the centre of Cardigan

🅿 Follow signs

**Distance and grade**

58 km (36 miles)

🢂🢂🢂 Moderate. The 11 km (7 mile) section alongside the River Cych southeast from Llechryd would make an easy 22 km (14 mile) there-and-back ride

The Teifi is one of the longest rivers in Wales, rising in the Cambrian mountains east of Aberystwyth and reaching the sea at Cardigan. The mouth of the estuary is followed north out of Cardigan with fine views out to the sea. A steep climb leads up to Ferwig. There are occasional glimpses of the sea from this road before it turns south near the unsightly buildings of the airfield. A short further climb takes you up and over back into the Teifi Valley at Llechryd. At this point, there is a short cut option back to the start. However, the best of the ride starts here as it follows the charming wooded valley of the Afon Cych for 11 km (7 miles) to the pub at Cwmcych. The second major climb of the ride, starting with a steep section, leads to the top of Rhos y llyn, the high point of the ride, with some magnificent views in all directions. Two long, downhill sections bring you back to Llechryd for a second time. The A484 back to Cardigan is avoided as much as possible by using minor and B roads.

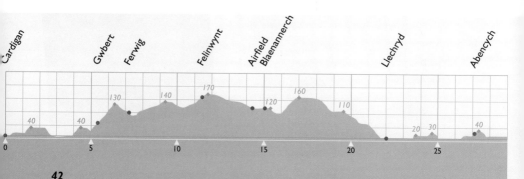

## Terrain

Two main climbs: the first divided into two parts – 130 m (430 ft) from the mouth of the Teifi to Ferwig and 85 m (280 ft) from Ferwig to Felinwynt; the second 200 m (650 ft) out of the Afon Cych Valley Rhos y llyn. Lowest point – sea level on the estuary of the Teifi. Highest point – 250 m (820 ft) at Rhos y llyn (instruction 13)

## Nearest railway

Whitland, 18 km (11 miles) south of Tegryn

## Refreshments

Eagle PH 🍺, plenty of choice, **Cardigan**
Carpenters Arms PH, **Llechryd**
Penrhiw Inn, Nags Head PH, **Abercych**
Fox & Hounds PH, **Cwmcych**
Butchers Arms PH, **Tegryn**
Boncath Inn, **Boncath**

## Places of interest

**Cardigan** 1
Market town at the mouth of the River Teifi. Cardigan's history goes back as far as 1136, becoming a major port in later centuries. There are old quayside warehouses around the 12th-century bridge, overlooked by a ruined medieval castle

**Cenarth** 11 (3 km (2 miles) off the route)
The River Teifi thunders towards an 18th-century bridge in a series of dramatic waterfalls. There is an old-world mill, stony cottages and a restored smithy. It is also the centre of coracle building – a curious fishing craft also used for racing

**Cilgerran** 18/19 (3 km (2 miles) off the route)
Set in a beautiful, wooded gorge, the village is one long street. The ruins of the 13th-century castle are perched on a wooded bluff above the River Teifi – the castle inspired one of Turner's finest works. Bison, wild boars and other rare breeds are to be found at the Cardigan Wildlife Park

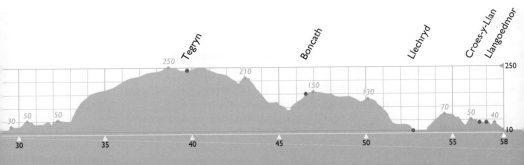

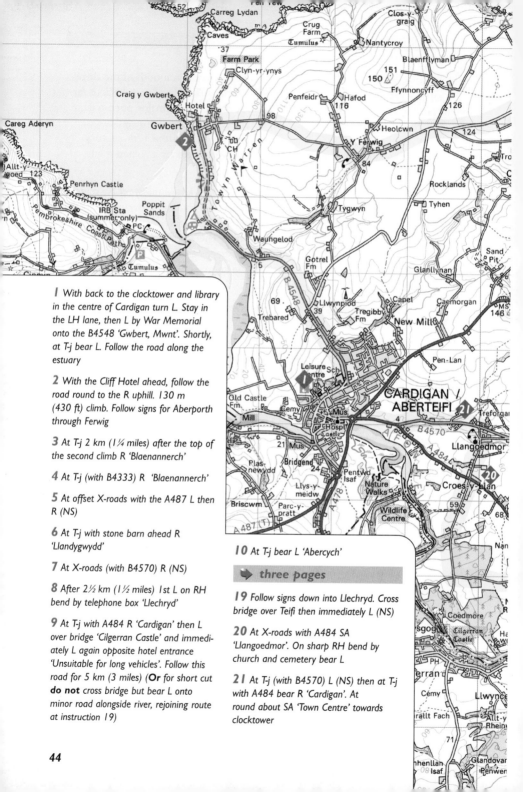

**1** With back to the clocktower and library in the centre of Cardigan turn L. Stay in the LH lane, then L by War Memorial onto the B4548 'Gwbert, Mwnt'. Shortly, at T-j bear L. Follow the road along the estuary

**2** With the Cliff Hotel ahead, follow the road round to the R uphill. 130 m (430 ft) climb. Follow signs for Aberporth through Ferwig

**3** At T-j 2 km (1¼ miles) after the top of the second climb R 'Blaenannerch'

**4** At T-j (with B4333) R 'Blaenannerch'

**5** At offset X-roads with the A487 L then R (NS)

**6** At T-j with stone barn ahead R 'Llandygwydd'

**7** At X-roads (with B4570) R (NS)

**8** After 2½ km (1½ miles) 1st L on RH bend by telephone box 'Llechryd'

**9** At T-j with A484 R 'Cardigan' then L over bridge 'Cilgerran Castle' and immediately L again opposite hotel entrance 'Unsuitable for long vehicles'. Follow this road for 5 km (3 miles) (**Or** for short cut **do not** cross bridge but bear L onto minor road alongside river, rejoining route at instruction 19)

**10** At T-j bear L 'Abercych'

➡ **three pages**

**19** Follow signs down into Llechryd. Cross bridge over Teifi then immediately L (NS)

**20** At X-roads with A484 SA 'Llangoedmor'. On sharp RH bend by church and cemetery bear L

**21** At T-j (with B4570) L (NS) then at T-j with A484 bear R 'Cardigan'. At round about SA 'Town Centre' towards clocktower

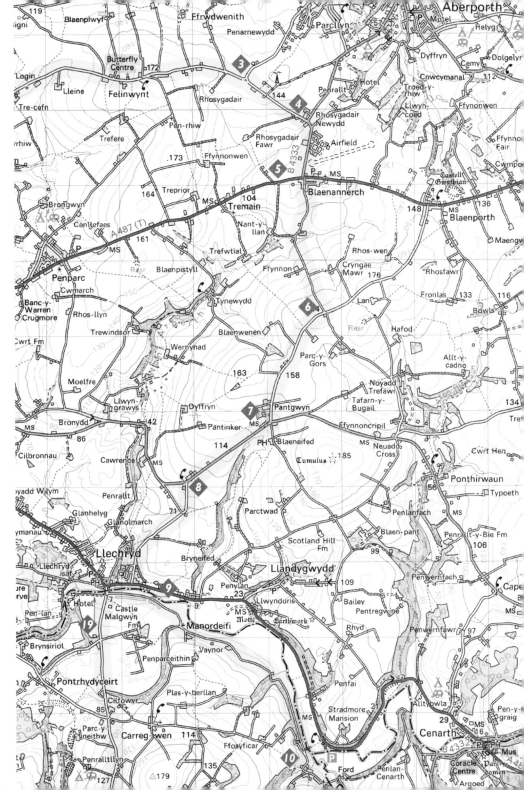

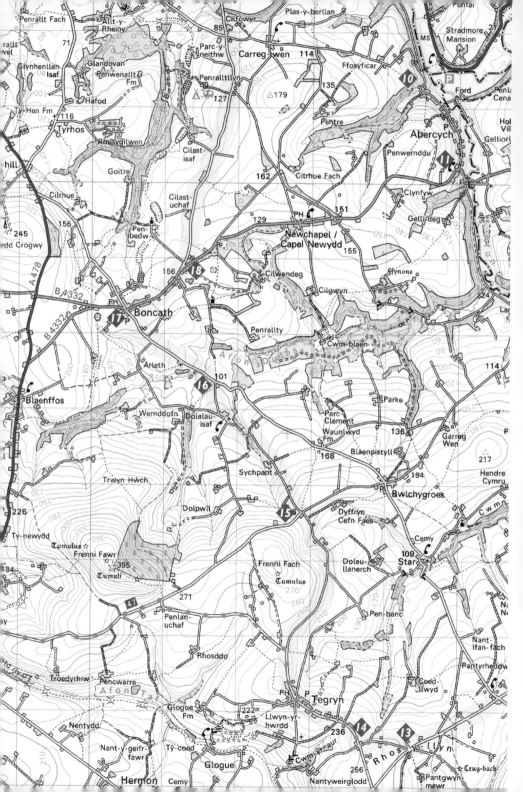

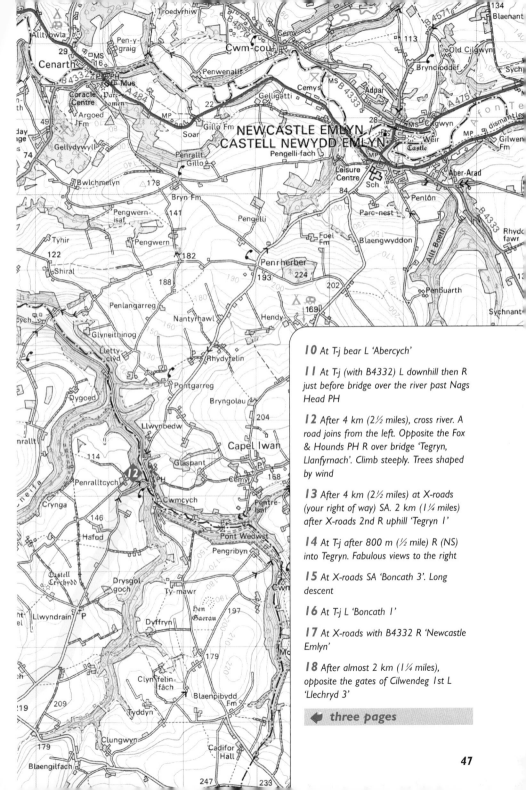

**10** At T-j bear L 'Abercych'

**11** At T-j (with B4332) L downhill then R just before bridge over the river past Nags Head PH

**12** After 4 km (2½ miles), cross river. A road joins from the left. Opposite the Fox & Hounds PH R over bridge 'Tegryn, Llanfyrnach'. Climb steeply. Trees shaped by wind

**13** After 4 km (2½ miles) at X-roads (your right of way) SA. 2 km (1¼ miles) after X-roads 2nd R uphill 'Tegryn 1'

**14** At T-j after 800 m (½ mile) R (NS) into Tegryn. Fabulous views to the right

**15** At X-roads SA 'Boncath 3'. Long descent

**16** At T-j L 'Boncath 1'

**17** At X-roads with B4332 R 'Newcastle Emlyn'

**18** After almost 2 km (1¼ miles), opposite the gates of Cilwendeg 1st L 'Llechryd 3'

◀ three pages

# 8 Along the coast from St David's to the Pen Caer Peninsula

The Pembrokeshire coastline is among Britain's finest, and time should be taken to make trips to the coast from St David's to see the rip tides of Ramsey Sound and the rocky promontory of St David's Head. Leaving the delights of St David's with its inspiring cathedral and the romantic ruins of the Bishop's Palace, this route follows the coast as closely as possible through a windswept and largely treeless landscape. The gorse strikes a bright yellow note in an otherwise grey setting. You touch the coast at Abercastle, formerly a busy trading port, and soon afterwards you have the choice of cutting the route short or continuing northwards to the hill fort of Garn Fawr. Take a lock with you so that you can leave your bike and climb to the top of the hill with its magnificent panoramic views. The return trip follows quiet inland lanes through Castlemorris and Middle Mill back to St David's.

## Start

The memorial cross in the centre of St David's

P Follow signs for long-stay car parks

## Distance and grade

60 km (37 miles) (short ride – 37 km (23 miles))

/// Moderate

## Terrain

Several climbs of 46–76 m (150–250 ft). One longer climb on the full-length route of 140 m (470 ft) (instructions 8/11). Lowest point – sea level at Abercastle. Highest point – 170 m (550 ft) on the road beneath Garn Fawr (instruction 11)

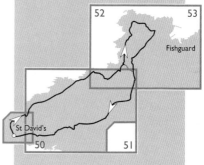

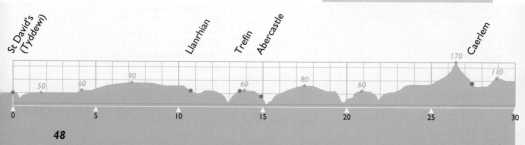

## Nearest railway

Goodwick/Fishguard, 3 km (2 miles) from the northern end of the route

## Refreshments

Farmers Arms PH 🍺, Old Cross PH, plenty of choice in **St David's**
Sloop Inn 🍺, **Porthgain** (just off the route)
Ship Inn, **Trefin**
Farmers Arms PH 🍺, **Mathry** (just off the route)
Y Gwesty Bach PH, **Castlemorris**
Cambrian Arms PH 🍺, Harbour House PH 🍺, **Solva** (just off the route)

## Places of interest

**St David's** *1*
Britain's smallest city. The magnificent cathedral was founded by St David, the patron saint of Wales, in the 6th century, and the bones in a casket behind the High Altar are believed to be his. The present cathedral was begun in the 12th century and shares its tranquil valley with the extensive ruins of the medieval Bishop's Palace

**Ramsey Island** *(ferry point at Porthstinian, 3 km (2 miles) west of St David's)*
This holy island was created, in legend, by a 6th-century Breton saint, Justinian, who axed it from the mainland to ensure solitude. There are summer boat trips from Porthstinian

**Whitesands Bay** *3 (3 km (2 miles) northwest of St David's)*
One of the finest surfing beaches on the Welsh coast and said to be the spot from which St Patrick sailed to Ireland

▼ *Fishguard Bay*

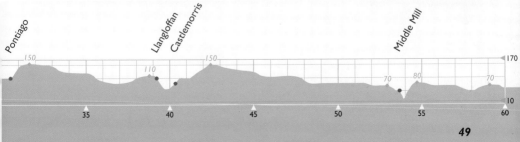

Pontiago · Llangloffan · Castlemorris · Middle Mill

150 · 110 · 150 · 70 · 80 · 70 · 170 · 10

35 · 40 · 45 · 50 · 55 · 60

**49**

**1** *From the memorial cross in the centre of St David's, take Main Street towards Fishguard (A487) and Whitesand (B4583). Ignore the 1st left on The Pebbles, take the next L onto Quickwell Hill*

**2** *Down hill, cross bridge, 1st R 'Whitesand 2'*

**3** *At X-roads (with B4583) SA (NS)*

**4** *Ignore left turns on No Through Roads. At T-j with stone-walled bank ahead L*

**5** *Follow this road for 12 km (7½ miles) through Llanrhian, Trefin and Abercastle*

➡ **two pages**

**17** *At next X-roads (Give Way) R (NS)*

**18** *Ignore turnings to right and left for 3½ km (2¼ miles). At T-j (with B4330) bear L then follow road to the R 'Penycwm, Llandeloy'*

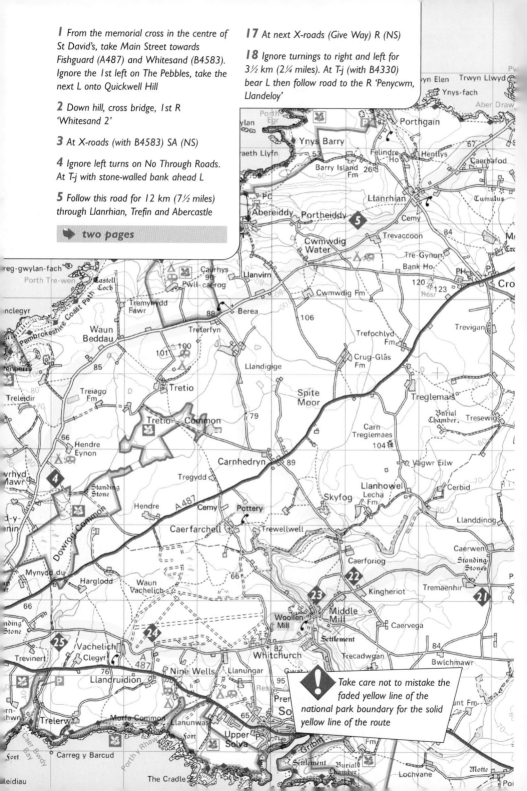

⚠ *Take care not to mistake the faded yellow line of the national park boundary for the solid yellow line of the route*

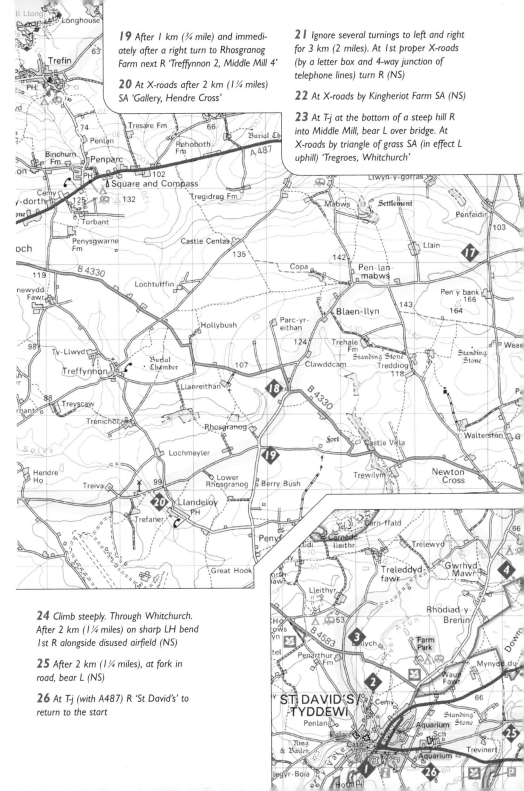

**19** After 1 km (¾ mile) and immediately after a right turn to Rhosgranog Farm next R 'Treffynnon 2, Middle Mill 4'

**20** At X-roads after 2 km (1¼ miles) SA 'Gallery, Hendre Cross'

**21** Ignore several turnings to left and right for 3 km (2 miles). At 1st proper X-roads (by a letter box and 4-way junction of telephone lines) turn R (NS)

**22** At X-roads by Kingheriot Farm SA (NS)

**23** At T-j at the bottom of a steep hill R into Middle Mill, bear L over bridge. At X-roads by triangle of grass SA (in effect L uphill) 'Tregroes, Whitchurch'

**24** Climb steeply. Through Whitchurch. After 2 km (1¼ miles) on sharp LH bend 1st R alongside disused airfield (NS)

**25** After 2 km (1¼ miles), at fork in road, bear L (NS)

**26** At T-j (with A487) R 'St David's' to return to the start

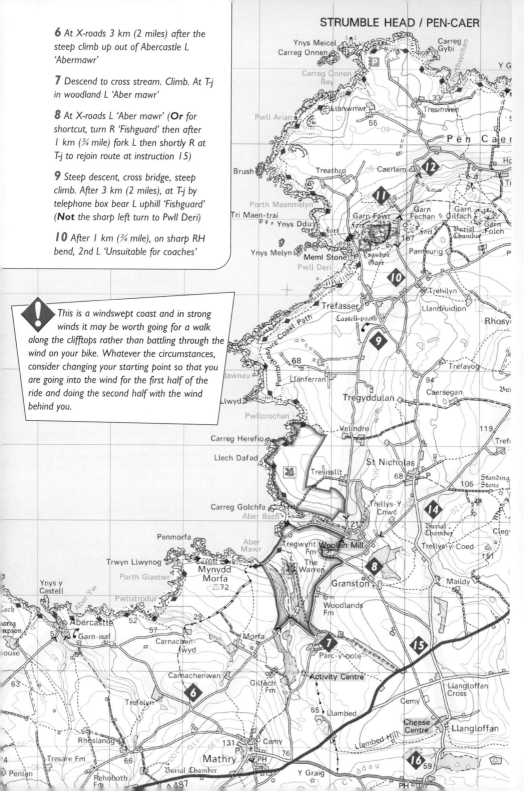

**6** At X-roads 3 km (2 miles) after the steep climb up out of Abercastle L 'Abermawr'

**7** Descend to cross stream. Climb. At T-j in woodland L 'Aber mawr'

**8** At X-roads L 'Aber mawr' (**Or** for shortcut, turn R 'Fishguard' then after 1 km (¾ mile) fork L then shortly R at T-j to rejoin route at instruction 15)

**9** Steep descent, cross bridge, steep climb. After 3 km (2 miles), at T-j by telephone box bear L uphill 'Fishguard' (**Not** the sharp left turn to Pwll Deri)

**10** After 1 km (¾ mile), on sharp RH bend, 2nd L 'Unsuitable for coaches'

This is a windswept coast and in strong winds it may be worth going for a walk along the clifftops rather than battling through the wind on your bike. Whatever the circumstances, consider changing your starting point so that you are going into the wind for the first half of the ride and doing the second half with the wind behind you.

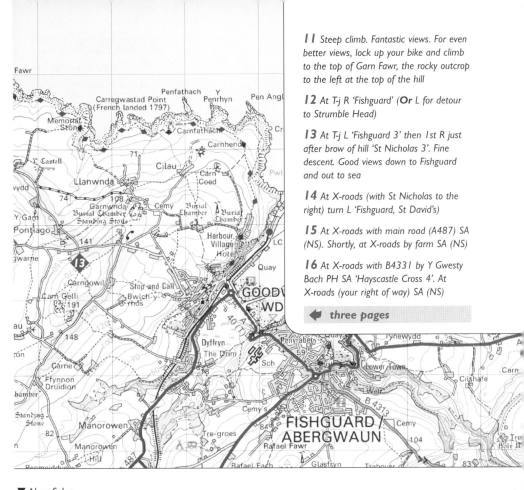

**11** *Steep climb. Fantastic views. For even better views, lock up your bike and climb to the top of Garn Fawr, the rocky outcrop to the left at the top of the hill*

**12** *At T-j R 'Fishguard' (**Or** L for detour to Strumble Head)*

**13** *At T-j L 'Fishguard 3' then 1st R just after brow of hill 'St Nicholas 3'. Fine descent. Good views down to Fishguard and out to sea*

**14** *At X-roads (with St Nicholas to the right) turn L 'Fishguard, St David's'*

**15** *At X-roads with main road (A487) SA (NS). Shortly, at X-roads by farm SA (NS)*

**16** *At X-roads with B4331 by Y Gwesty Bach PH SA 'Hayscastle Cross 4'. At X-roads (your right of way) SA (NS)*

◀ **three pages**

▼ *Near Solva*

# 9 West from Haverfordwest to the coast at Nolton Haven

Haverfordwest is the hub from which roads radiate to the various corners of Pembrokeshire and as such it has a dispro-portionate amount of traffic for a town of its size. There is an attractive pedestrian-ised heart to the town inside the ring road. Exits to the west are not ideal but as soon as you leave the B4341 at Portfield Gate the character of the ride changes entirely. Small quiet lanes lead west to the coast at Nolton Haven with wide-ranging views out to the sea. The stretch along Newgale sands is a delight, unlike the short, steep section on the A487, which must be tackled before plunging once again into the network of Pembrokeshire lanes. Away from the coast, the land softens and there are more trees and hedgerows. The Western Cleddau River is crossed at Wolf's Castle as the ride turns south and follows ever narrower, less frequented lanes. A final descent drops you at the roundabout by the Tourist Information Centre in the centre of Haverfordwest, a different world from the lanes you have just explored.

## Start

The Tourist Information Centre (near the bus station), Haverfordwest

P There is a long-stay car park just off the dual carriageway/ring road leading away from the roundabout nearest to the Tourist Information Centre towards the A40 east (Camarthen)

## Distance and grade

45 km (28 miles)

Moderate

## Refreshments

Bristol Trader PH ☻, George PH ☻, plenty of choice in **Haverfordwest**
Mariners Arms PH, **Nolton Haven**
Duke of Edinburgh PH, **Newgale**
Cross Inn, **Hayscastle Cross**
The Wolfe PH ☻, **Wolfe's Castle**

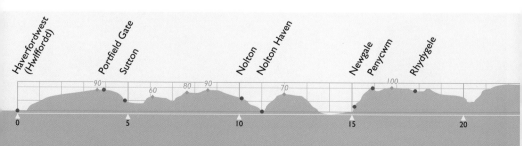

## Terrain

Several short climbs of 46–76 m (150–250 ft), two longer ones – 91 m (300 ft) from the start to Portfield Gate with a steep section in Haverfordwest itself; 100 m (330 ft) up from the coast at Newgale, a steep and busy section. Lowest point – sea level at Haverfordwest, Nolton Haven and Newgale. Highest point – 120 m (385 ft) at Hayscastle Cross

## Nearest railway

Haverfordwest

## Places of interest

### The Landsker

The Landsker, or 'land scar', is a ghostly line running from Amroth, east of Tenby across to Newgale on the west coast, its route marked by a series of ruined castles. Although it does not appear on any official map, its historic influence has been profound. It originates from the Norman invasion of West Wales in the 11th century. The native Welsh population retreated to the north, blocked off from the south by a string of Norman castles. English ways, customs and language subsequently gripped the south, turning it into the 'Little England beyond Wales'. The divisions that it has created are summed up in the place names that straddle the 'border'

▲ Near Newgale

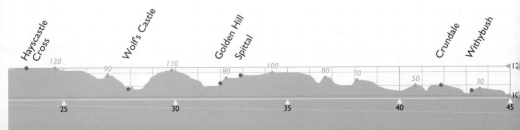

**1** With back to the entrance of the Tourist Information Centre L and L again past the public conveniences and through the car park to the far end. Continue in same direction passing an elevated foot-bridge to your left then bear L towards tall brick wall

**2** At pavement, dismount for 50 m (yd), walking past County Hotel then turn R onto the High Street, crossing the bridge and climbing past Castle Hotel on the one-way system

**3** At top of hill, get into RH lane by the traffic lights and Post Office 'Dale, Broad Haven' then shortly bear L (in effect SA) 'Dale B4327, Broad Haven (B4341)'

**4** Shortly after the sign at the start of the village of Portfield Gate, turn R by Penry Arms PH 'Sutton'

**5** In Sutton bear R (in effect SA) by bus shelter 'Pelcomb 1½, Nolton 3' then bear L. Follow signs for Nolton turning L shortly after Bethel Baptist Chapel

⇒ **two pages**

**15** At T-j on U-bend bear L (in effect SA). Cross bridge. At T-j L over 2nd bridge then 1st R sharply back on yourself 'Spittal 1'. Climb hill

**16** At offset X-roads R then L (NS). At T-j after 100 m (yd) L (NS) past St Mary's Church

**17** At X-roads (with B4329) SA 'Walton East 3, Clarbeston Road 2½'

**18** Descend, cross stream, climb. 1st R '15 ft 6 in height limit'

**19** Beneath two bridges. At T-j R

**20** At T-j (with B4329) L (NS)

**21** At roundabout SA 'Haverfordwest'

**22** At T-j bear L. At roundabout SA 'St Davids, Bus Station' then 1st L to return to Tourist Information Centre

Take care not to mistake the faded yellow line of the national park boundary for the solid yellow line of the route

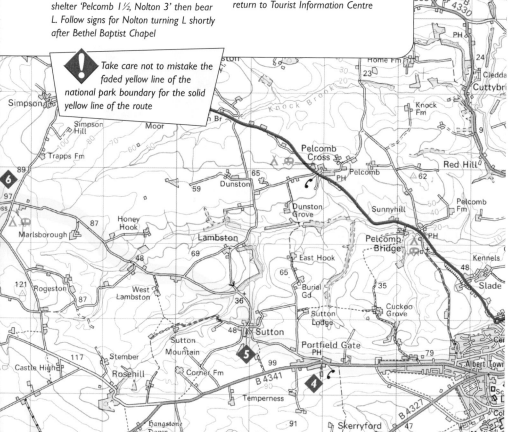

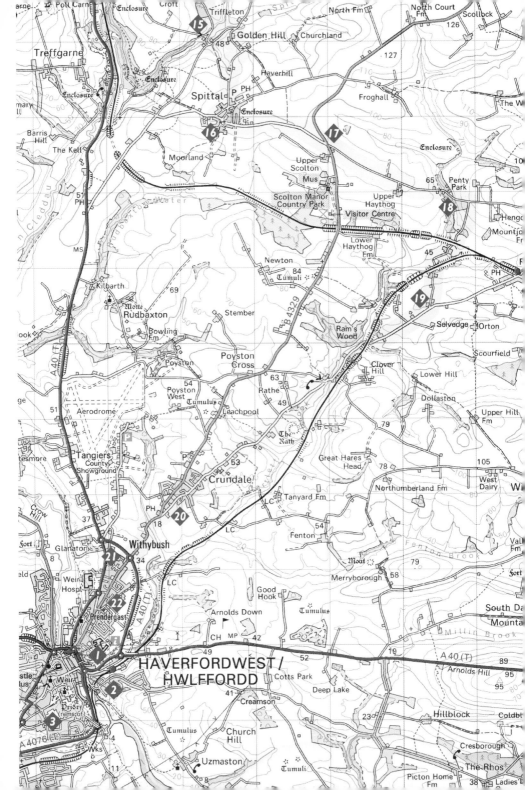

**6** At X-roads (your right of way) at Nolton Cross SA 'Nolton Haven'. Climb up from Nolton then descend to the beach again

**7** At T-j with A487 by triangle of grass bear L (in effect SA) (NS). Unpleasant climb on unpleasant road

**8** Shortly after the brow of hill 1st R 'Trefgarn Owen 2, Llandeloy 3, Mathry 6'

**9** Shortly after airfield on sharp LH bend bear R (in effect SA) (NS). Ignore left and right turns, drop steeply to cross stream then climb steeply on the other side

**!** Take care not to mistake the faded yellow line of the national park boundary for the solid yellow line of the route

Mountain Park
Tr
Ffynnon Gron
Pont-yr-hafod
Haycastle
Hayscastle Cross PH
11
10
11
Broad
Hayscastle Tump
Pen-y-gors
Cemy
Asheston Ho
109
Rickeston Hall
Trefgarn Owen
117
Brandy Bro
Brawdy Airfield (disused)
9
Troed-y-rhiw
41
Gignog
Standing Stone
113
Broad
Rhydygele
Knaveston
73
Tumulus
Rhyndaston-fawr
Tanybryn
Mounta Co
Sort
72
Ford
Settlement
Little Rhyndaston
Tu
Brawdy Fm
Eweston
Barch
116
178
Plums Mou
Llethr
89
Rhyndaston Mountain
125
Dudwell Mountain
8
Penycwm
90
Slade
70
Enclosure
146
Cuffern Mountain
150
Newgale Fm
30
Bramble
12
Ferny Glen
Rock Fm
108
Newgale
PH
Roch Br
Woodhawk
7
Wood
65
Southwood
PH
Roch
Castle
67
Cuffern
Dudwells
Roblesto Hal
Church Hill
Roch Gate
105
56
Stock Park Fm
P
PC
27
Motel
96
Scamford
aidenhall Point
P
Trefrane
Hil
Chy
79
Folly
75
81
Simpson
114
Mus
74
Keeston
Cemy
53
Slad Fm
Scamford
ss
Black Cliff
Folkeston Hill
Rickets Head
Simpson Hill
Keeston Moor
Keeston Br
PH
P
Nolton Haven
Cemy
Trapps Fm
Nolton Haven
Madoc's Haven
57
Nolton
68
Longlands
89
6
59
Dunston
97
65
Nolton Cross
Honey Hook
27
87

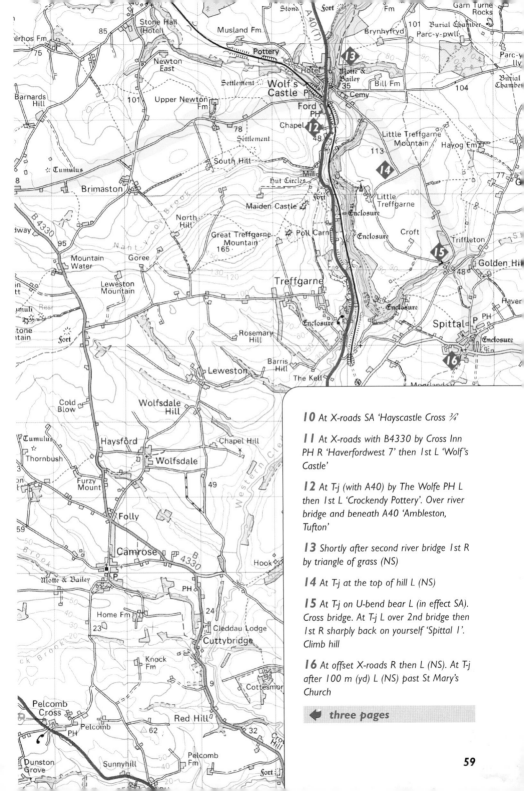

**10** At X-roads SA 'Hayscastle Cross ¾'

**11** At X-roads with B4330 by Cross Inn PH R 'Haverfordwest 7' then 1st L 'Wolf's Castle'

**12** At T-j (with A40) by The Wolfe PH L then 1st L 'Crockendy Pottery'. Over river bridge and beneath A40 'Ambleston, Tufton'

**13** Shortly after second river bridge 1st R by triangle of grass (NS)

**14** At T-j at the top of hill L (NS)

**15** At T-j on U-bend bear L (in effect SA). Cross bridge. At T-j L over 2nd bridge then 1st R sharply back on yourself 'Spittal 1'. Climb hill

**16** At offset X-roads R then L (NS). At T-j after 100 m (yd) L (NS) past St Mary's Church

◀ *three pages*

# 10 *Along the coast, south of Pembroke*

The predominance of English names in the area testifies to the invasion by the Normans in the 12th century and their invitation to Flemish traders to come and settle here. Climbs in and out of the extensive estuary of Milford Haven take you to the spectacular castle at Carew and on to the lovely wooded setting of Cresswell Quay. The ride turns inland and through the pretty village of St Florence before reaching the coast at Manorbier. The coastline is followed as closely as possible for several kilometres, through the dubious charms of Freshwater East and the undeniable ones of the woodlands and lily ponds between Stack-pole and Bosh-erton. Two side trips from the main route are highly recommended: to the chapel and cliffs at St Govan's Head and to the impressive limestone rocks of Elegug Stacks, surrounded by wheeling seabirds.

## Start

The Tourist Information Centre, Pembroke

P Opposite the Tourist Information Centre

## Distance and grade

48 km (30 miles). The side trip to St Govan's Head is an extra 10 km (6 miles). To Elegug Stacks 5 km (3 miles)

*Moderate*

## Terrain

There are 8 climbs of 46–91 m (150–300 ft), some of them with steep sections. Lowest point – sea level at several points. Highest point – 85 m (280 ft) at the crossroads on The Ridgeway above Manorbier

## Nearest railway

Pembroke

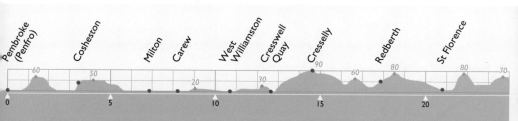

### Pembroke 1
Has one of the largest and most impressive Norman castles in Britain, standing on a promontory in the Pembroke River and ringed with walls and towers. The keep is 23 m (75 ft) high. It is also the reputed birthplace of Henry VIII in 1457

### Carew Castle 7
Magnificent ruins of a 13th-century castle built by Sir Nicholas de Carew, with Tudor additions. The rise and fall of the tide on the Carew River powers a 19th-century tidal mill, the only one of its kind in Wales still left intact. Carew's other treasure is a magnificent Celtic cross that stands beside the road near the inn. Almost 4 m (14 ft) high and carved with intricate geometrical patterns, it is believed to date from the 11th century and is one of the finest in Europe

### Elegug Stacks 29
(just off the route) The massive limestone pillars owe their name to nesting guillemots ('heligog' in Welsh). An official bird sanctuary, famous for razorbills, kittiwakes and fulmars

▼ *Elegug Stacks*

Watermans Arms PH 🍺, plenty of choice in **Pembroke**
Parsonage Farm Inn, Sun Inn, New Inn, **St Florence**
Ye Olde Worlde Cafe, St Govans Inn 🍺, **Bosherton**
Bramley Tea Rooms in plant nursery (17/18)
Cresselly Arms PH 🍺🍺, **Cresswell Quay**
Castle Inn, Chives Tea Room, **Manorbier**
Hill House Inn, Brewery Inn, **Cosheston**
Armstrong Arms PH 🍺🍺, **Stackpole**
Milton Brewery PH, **Milton**
Freshwater Inn, **Freshwater**
Carew Inn 🍺🍺, **Carew**

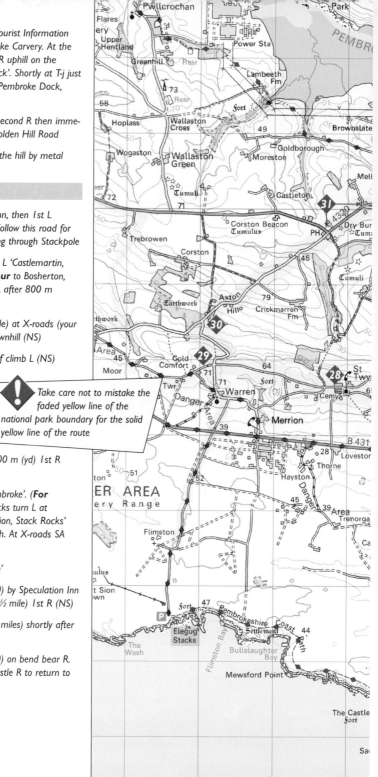

**1** With back to the Tourist Information Centre R past Pembroke Carvery. At the end of the road bear R uphill on the B4139 'Pembroke Dock'. Shortly at T-j just before clock tower L 'Pembroke Dock, Milford Haven'

**2** Cross bridge, take second R then immediately L at T-j onto Golden Hill Road

**3** At T-j at the top of the hill by metal railings bear R (NS)

➡ **two pages**

**24** Past Freshwater Inn, then 1st L 'Trewent, Stackpole'. Follow this road for 6 km (4 miles), passing through Stackpole

**25** At T-j with B4319 L 'Castlemartin, Bosherton'. (**For detour** to Bosherton, St Govan's Head 1st L after 800 m (½ mile) 'Bosherton')

**26** After 1 km (¾ mile) at X-roads (your right of way) 1st R downhill (NS)

**27** At T-j at the top of climb L (NS)

**28** At T-j by church in St Twynnells R (NS) then shortly at T-j with Woodland Rise L 'Warren, Castlemartin'. After 200 m (yd) 1st R 'Castlemartin'

Take care not to mistake the faded yellow line of the national park boundary for the solid yellow line of the route

**29** At X-roads R 'Pembroke'. (**For detour** to Elegug Stacks turn L at X-roads 'Warren, Marion, Stack Rocks' then 1st R after church. At X-roads SA over grid)

**30** At T-j R 'Pembroke'

**31** At T-j (with B4320) by Speculation Inn R (NS). After 800 m (½ mile) 1st R (NS)

**32** After 2½ km (1½ miles) shortly after two right turns, 2nd L

**33** At T-j (with B4320) on bend bear R. At next T-j, beneath castle R to return to the start

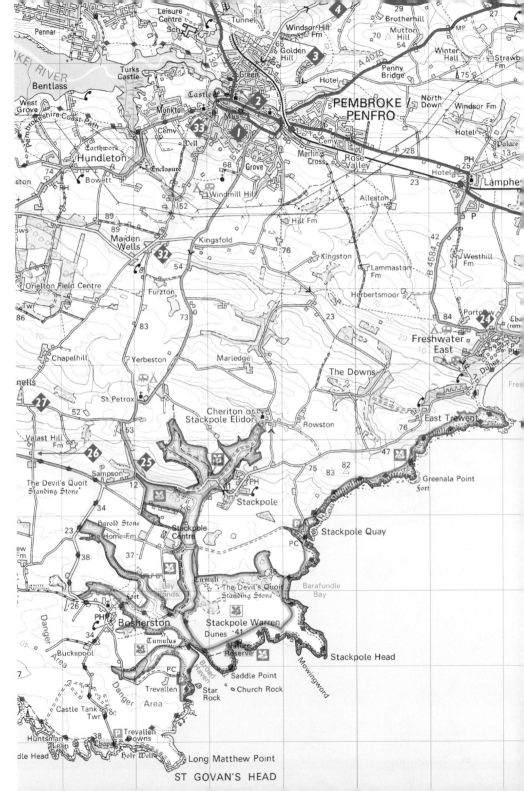

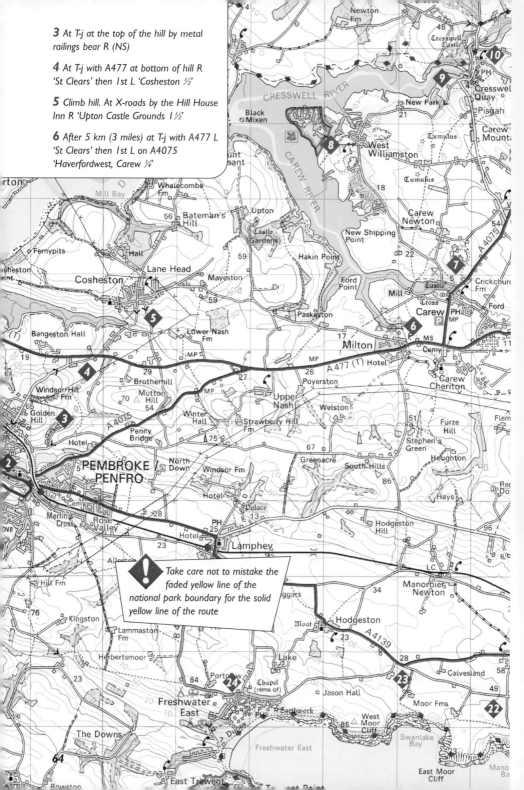

**3** At T-j at the top of the hill by metal railings bear R (NS)

**4** At T-j with A477 at bottom of hill R 'St Clears' then 1st L 'Cosheston ½'

**5** Climb hill. At X-roads by the Hill House Inn R 'Upton Castle Grounds 1½'

**6** After 5 km (3 miles) at T-j with A477 L 'St Clears' then 1st L on A4075 'Haverfordwest, Carew ¼'

Take care not to mistake the faded yellow line of the national park boundary for the solid yellow line of the route

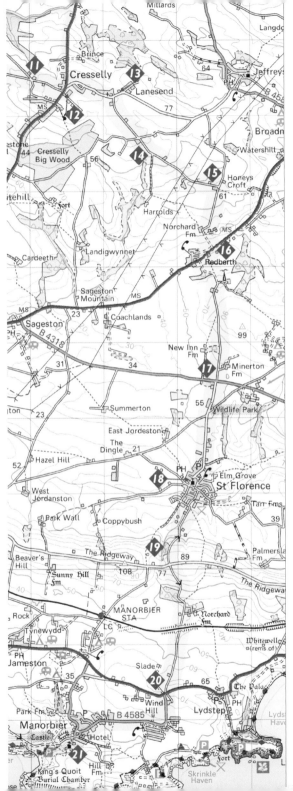

**7** Cross estuary then 1st L 'West Williamston 1½'

**8** At X-roads by telephone box in West Williamston SA (NS)

**9** At T-j on steep hill bear L downhill (NS)

**10** Shortly after passing Cresselly Arms PH in Cresswell Quay 1st R 'Cresselly'

**11** Climb hill. At T-j by triangle of grass and lamppost bear R uphill (NS)

**12** At offset X-roads with A4075 L then R 'Jeffreyston'

**13** 800 m (½ mile) after Primitive Methodist Chapel to the left 1st R by triangle of grass 'Redberth'

**14** At X-roads by farmhouse SA 'Redberth'

**15** At T-j R 'Redberth'

**16** At T-j (with A477) R 'St Florence 2' then 1st L 'St Florence'

**17** At X-roads (with B4318) SA 'St Florence ¾'

**18** Follow signs for Manorbier round one-way system turning L downhill at X-roads to go past New Inn

**19** Steep climb. At X-roads SA 'Riding Stables'

**20** At X-roads (with A4139) SA onto B4585 'Manorbier 1, Skrinkle Haven 1½'

**21** Through Manorbier bearing L soon after Castle Inn 'Car Park, Beach, Castle'. Descend past castle to beach. Fine sea views. Steep climb

**22** At X-roads L (NS)

**23** At T-j with main road (A4139) bear L (in effect SA) then shortly 1st L

**24** Past Freshwater Inn, then 1st L 'Trewent, Stackpole'. Follow this road for 6 km (4 miles), passing through Stackpole

◀ **three pages**

65

# Down to the coast southwest of Carmarthen

**Start**

The War Memorial near the Tourist Information Centre in Lammas Street, Carmarthen

🅿 Follow signs. There is a one-way system in Carmarthen, so you may have to dismount and progress on foot for short sections to get to the start

Carmarthen's one-way system and pedestrianised areas are a little confusing for the first-time visitor to the town and you should be prepared to walk rather than cycle for short sections if necessary. The exit from the town to the northwest is on a superbly graded lane that climbs steadily for 10 km (6 miles) through woodlands and banked hedgerows to the high point of the ride east of Talog. From here onwards, the climbs are shorter, steeper and more closely spaced. Heading south on the B4299, the views suddenly open up in a spectacular fashion above Meidrim. Crossing the A40 gives you the impression of leaving the mainland to find yourself on an island, so cut-off this area appears to be. Tiny lanes climb steeply past whitewashed cottages and farms as you head south down through the peninsula to Llansteffan with its castle, pubs and estuary views. The estuary is followed northeast, climbing to Llangain before the descent back down into Carmarthen.

**Distance and grade**

48 km (30 miles)

Moderate/strenuous

**Terrain**

Steady, well-graded climb of 210 m (700 ft) over 10 km (6½ miles) from the start to the high point of the ride. 91 m (300 ft) climb between Talog and Pen-y-bont. 91-m (300 ft) climb between Morfa Bach and

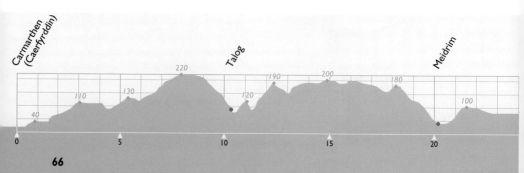

Llangain. Several shorter climbs throughout the ride. Lowest point – sea level in Carmarthen and at Llansteffan. Highest point – 210 m (700 ft) between Bwlchnewydd and Talog

Carmarthen

▼ Llansteffan

## Places of interest

### Carmarthen 1

Built on the banks of the River Tywi, the town is rich in Arthurian connections and is especially renowned as the legendary haunt of Merlin the Magician. 'Merlin's Cave' is near to the Museum of Carmarthen at Abergwili, 3 km (2 miles) east from the centre of town on the A40. There is also a Roman amphitheatre, one of only seven of its kind in Britain and built 2000 years ago when Carmarthen was known as Moridunum

### Llansteffan 17

Small but elegant Victorian and Georgian houses line the narrow main street, climbing towards a little square shared by two inns and the former village pound, now a shop. The 12th-century church is Norman with a lofty tower. The Green, which overlooks the shore, is dominated by the romantic ruins of Llansteffan's castle, also built by the Normans. Set high above the beach on a wooded headland, it inspired innumer-

## Refreshments

*Plenty of choice in* **Carmarthen**
*Sticks Hotel, Castle Inn,* **Llansteffan**
*Panty Y Dderwen PH,* **Llangain**
*Maenllwyd PH 🍺, (1 km (¾ mile) west of village), Fountain Inn, New Inn,* **Meidrim**
*Fox & Hounds PH,* **Bancyfelin**

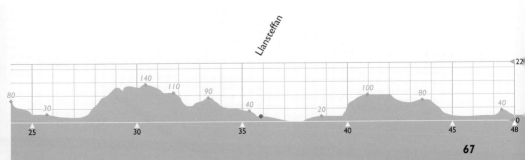

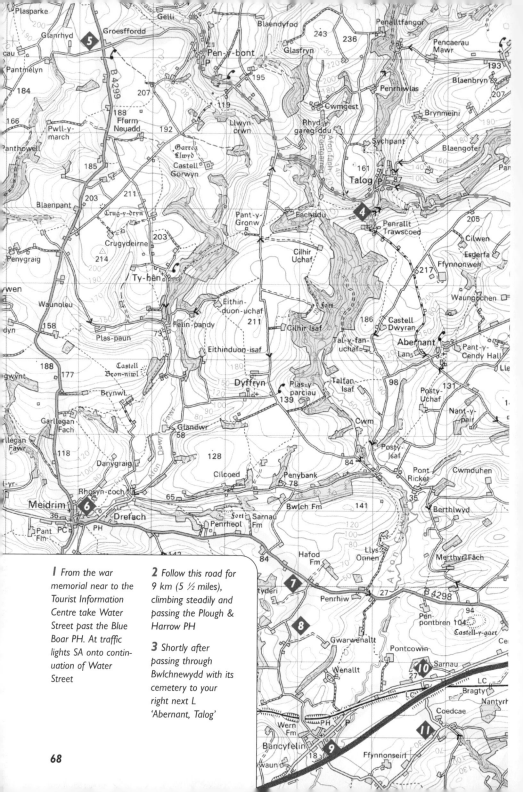

**1** From the war memorial near to the Tourist Information Centre take Water Street past the Blue Boar PH. At traffic lights SA onto continuation of Water Street

**2** Follow this road for 9 km (5 ½ miles), climbing steadily and passing the Plough & Harrow PH

**3** Shortly after passing through Bwlchnewydd with its cemetery to your right next L 'Abernant, Talog'

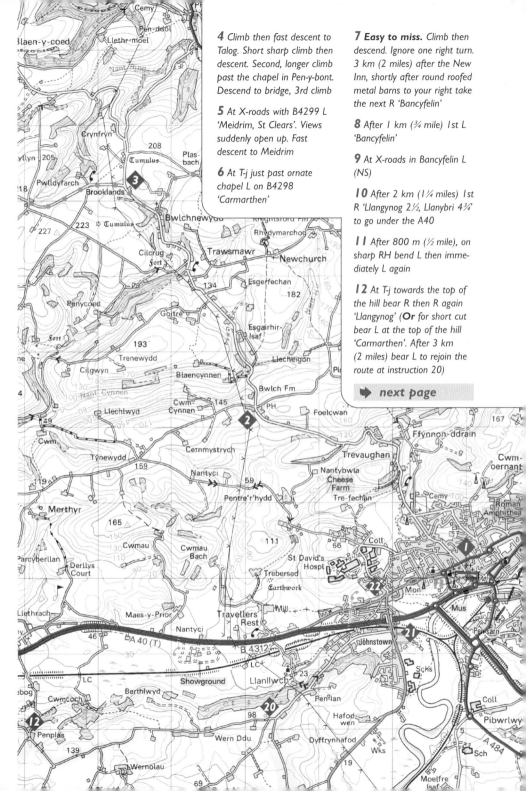

**4** Climb then fast descent to Talog. Short sharp climb then descent. Second, longer climb past the chapel in Pen-y-bont. Descend to bridge, 3rd climb

**5** At X-roads with B4299 L 'Meidrim, St Clears'. Views suddenly open up. Fast descent to Meidrim

**6** At T-j just past ornate chapel L on B4298 'Carmarthen'

**7** **Easy to miss.** Climb then descend. Ignore one right turn. 3 km (2 miles) after the New Inn, shortly after round roofed metal barns to your right take the next R 'Bancyfelin'

**8** After 1 km (¾ mile) 1st L 'Bancyfelin'

**9** At X-roads in Bancyfelin L (NS)

**10** After 2 km (1¼ miles) 1st R 'Llangynog 2½, Llanybri 4¾' to go under the A40

**11** After 800 m (½ mile), on sharp RH bend L then immediately L again

**12** At T-j towards the top of the hill bear R then R again 'Llangynog' (**Or** for short cut bear L at the top of the hill 'Carmarthen'. After 3 km (2 miles) bear L to rejoin the route at instruction 20)

➡ next page

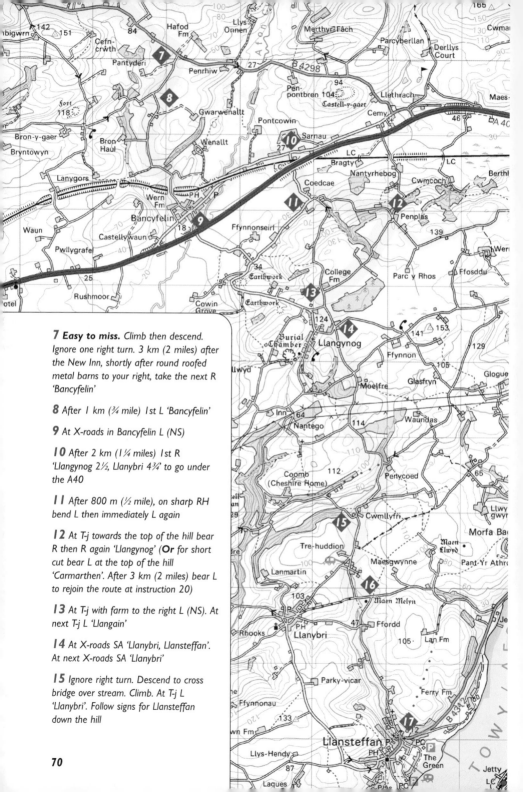

**7 Easy to miss.** Climb then descend. Ignore one right turn. 3 km (2 miles) after the New Inn, shortly after round roofed metal barns to your right, take the next R 'Bancyfelin'

**8** After 1 km (¾ mile) 1st L 'Bancyfelin'

**9** At X-roads in Bancyfelin L (NS)

**10** After 2 km (1¼ miles) 1st R 'Llangynog 2½, Llanybri 4¾' to go under the A40

**11** After 800 m (½ mile), on sharp RH bend L then immediately L again

**12** At T-j towards the top of the hill bear R then R again 'Llangynog' (**Or** for short cut bear L at the top of the hill 'Carmarthen'. After 3 km (2 miles) bear L to rejoin the route at instruction 20)

**13** At T-j with farm to the right L (NS). At next T-j L 'Llangain'

**14** At X-roads SA 'Llanybri, Llansteffan'. At next X-roads SA 'Llanybri'

**15** Ignore right turn. Descend to cross bridge over stream. Climb. At T-j L 'Llanybri'. Follow signs for Llansteffan down the hill

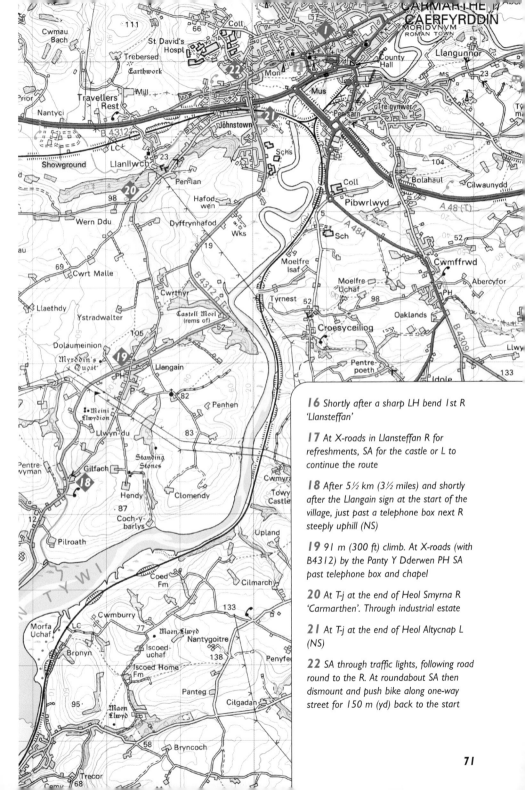

**16** Shortly after a sharp LH bend 1st R 'Llansteffan'

**17** At X-roads in Llansteffan R for refreshments, SA for the castle or L to continue the route

**18** After 5½ km (3½ miles) and shortly after the Llangain sign at the start of the village, just past a telephone box next R steeply uphill (NS)

**19** 91 m (300 ft) climb. At X-roads (with B4312) by the Panty Y Dderwen PH SA past telephone box and chapel

**20** At T-j at the end of Heol Smyrna R 'Carmarthen'. Through industrial estate

**21** At T-j at the end of Heol Altycnap L (NS)

**22** SA through traffic lights, following road round to the R. At roundabout SA then dismount and push bike along one-way street for 150 m (yd) back to the start

# 12 *South from Carmarthen to Kidwelly and the Tywi Estuary*

The second of the two rides that start from Carmarthen, this one climbs to the east above the valley formed by the River Tywi with fine views of the rounded hills to the north. You drop down into a second river valley of the Gwendraeth Fach, which is followed for 14 km (9 miles), climbing to the quarries near Crwbin and through fertile farming country before the long and gentle descent into Kidwelly with its spec-tacular castle. The only drawback along the delightful stretch of the Tywi Estuary coastline is the existence of a caravan site near to St Ishmael that may bring cars and caravans on to this narrow lane at busy holiday times. The views across the estuary to Llansteffan are wonderful. A steep climb takes you up and away from the coast and back to Carmarthen.

74  Carmarthen  75

76  Kidwelly  77

## Start

The bridge over the Tywi, beneath County Hall, Carmarthen

P  Follow signs

## Distance and grade

51 km (32 miles)

/// Moderate

## Terrain

Three main climbs – 100 m (330 ft) at the start, east from Carmarthen; 119 m (390 ft) west from Porthyrhyd; 137 m (450 ft) up from the coast at Ferryside. Lowest point – sea level at Carmarthen, Kidwelly and Ferryside. Highest point – 170 m (550 ft) between Porthyrhyd and Crwbin

## Nearest railway

Carmarthen

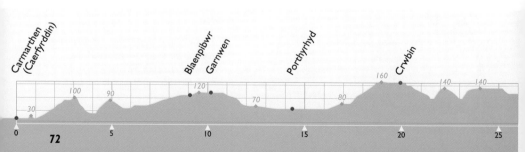

Carmarthen (Caerfyrddin) · Blaenpibwr · Garnwen · Porthyrhyd · Crwbin

30 · 100 · 90 · 120 · 70 · 80 · 160 · 140 · 140

0 · 5 · 10 · 15 · 20 · 25

## Places of interest

### Kidwelly 15

Town dominated by the well-preserved, 12th-century castle with massive towers. Below, the 14th-century bridge spans the little Gwendraeth Fach River. The Gothic church dates from the late 13th century and once served a Benedictine monastery. The industrial museum displays the 18th-century machinery used for tinplate manufacturing. Founded in 1737, the Kidwelly tinplate works grew into one of the largest during the booming 19th century

### Ferryside 18/19

Peaceful coastal village on the banks of the River Tywi with scenic coast-hugging railway line. The Tywi flows through sandbanks and cockle and mussel beds into Carmarthen Bay

## Refreshments

Plenty of choice in **Carmarthen**
Abadam Arms PH, Prince of Wales PH, **Porthyrhyd**
Plenty of choice in **Kidwelly**

◀ Kidwelly Castle

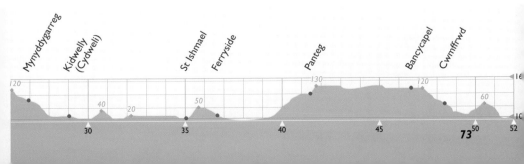

**73**

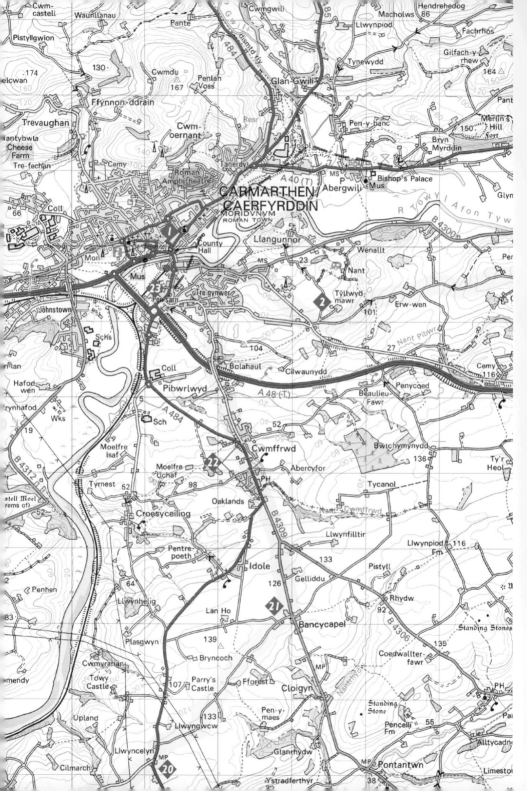

**1** From beneath County Hall, cross the bridge over the River Tywi away from town. At roundabout 1st L on to B4300 'Llangunnor'. Climb hill, ignoring left turn on B4300, passing mast and Police HQ on your left

**2** Shortly after hire centre 1st L (NS)

**3** At T-j R 'Llanddarog 2½' then after 1 km (¾ mile), immediately after chapel on right, 1st L 'Nantgaredig 2'

**4** At T-j R (NS). After 1 km (¾ mile) 1st L (NS)

**5** At T-j with B4310 R 'Porthyrhyd 2'

**6** At T-j with Abadam Arms PH ahead L then 1st R immediately after cemetery

**7** At T-j after 3 km (2 miles) L uphill 'Crwbin 1¾'. Follow signs for Crwbin ignoring fork to right

**8** At X-roads (with B4306) by telephone box SA past wooden bench (NS) (**Or** R downhill for shortcut, rejoining route at instructions 21/22)

➡ **two pages**

**20** At T-j with main road (A484) by stone barns L (NS) then shortly 1st R

**21** At X-roads (with B4309) L (NS)

**22** At T-j with A484 R 'Carmarthen'. Past Black Lion Inn and church. 1st R onto Bolahaul Road. (The A484 is a **busy road**, so pull in to the left and check the road is clear before turning right)

**23** At T-j with shopping warehouses ahead R (NS). At roundabout SA to return to start

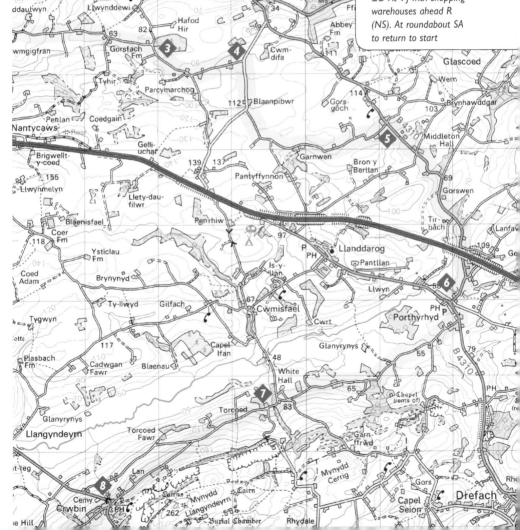

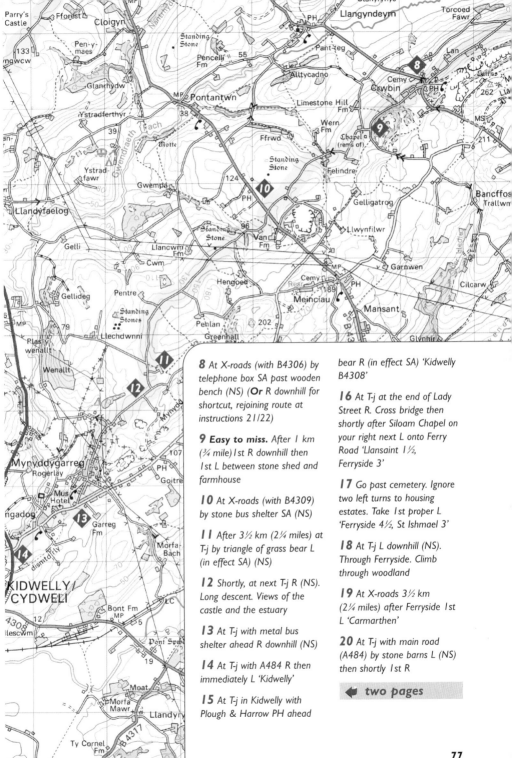

**8** At X-roads (with B4306) by telephone box SA past wooden bench (NS) (**Or** R downhill for shortcut, rejoining route at instructions 21/22)

**9** *Easy to miss.* After 1 km (¾ mile) 1st R downhill then 1st L between stone shed and farmhouse

**10** At X-roads (with B4309) by stone bus shelter SA (NS)

**11** After 3½ km (2¼ miles) at T-j by triangle of grass bear L (in effect SA) (NS)

**12** Shortly, at next T-j R (NS). Long descent. Views of the castle and the estuary

**13** At T-j with metal bus shelter ahead R downhill (NS)

**14** At T-j with A484 R then immediately L 'Kidwelly'

**15** At T-j in Kidwelly with Plough & Harrow PH ahead

bear R (in effect SA) 'Kidwelly B4308'

**16** At T-j at the end of Lady Street R. Cross bridge then shortly after Siloam Chapel on your right next L onto Ferry Road 'Llansaint 1½, Ferryside 3'

**17** Go past cemetery. Ignore two left turns to housing estates. Take 1st proper L 'Ferryside 4½, St Ishmael 3'

**18** At T-j L downhill (NS). Through Ferryside. Climb through woodland

**19** At X-roads 3½ km (2¼ miles) after Ferryside 1st L 'Carmarthen'

**20** At T-j with main road (A484) by stone barns L (NS) then shortly 1st R

◀ **two pages**

# 13 East from Abergavenny to Raglan

**Start**

The Baptist Church / War Memorial at the end of the High Street, Abergavenny

🅿 Large, free car park on the central ring road, opposite super-markets, close to the start

**Distance and grade**

48 km (30 miles)

/// Moderate

**A**bergavenny is in many ways the gateway to the Welsh mountains from the east. It is surrounded by three distinctively shaped hills: the Skirrid, the Blorenge and the Sugar Loaf, and during the course of the ride there are fine views of all three and of many others besides. You start climbing right from the beginning of the ride and then descend to run parallel with the noisy A40 for a brief stretch before Raglan. A visit to the well-preserved, atmospheric castle in Raglan is highly recommended. The old A40 (now a yellow road) is surprisingly busy, hence the twists and turns to avoid it west of Raglan. Three climbs to the north and then to the west take you back up onto the rolling hills near Llantilio Crossenny and Cross Ash with magnificent views opening up. The ridge ride up over Campston Hill is particularly memorable. A fast descent to Llanivangel Crucorney takes you past an excellent old pub. The last gentle climb to Pantygelli sets you up for a fine, exhilarating descent down into Abergavenny.

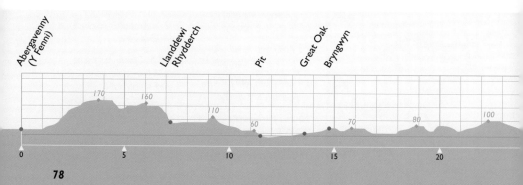

## 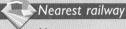Terrain

Four main climbs –
120 m (400 ft) climb at
the start east from
Abergavenny, 120 m
(400 ft) climb north
from Llantilio
Crossenny, 91 m
(300 ft) climb near
Cross Ash with one
steep section, 85 m
(280 ft) climb to the
highpoint on Campston
Hill. Lowest point –
50 m (165 ft) in
Abergavenny and
Raglan. Highest point –
270 m (900 ft) at the
top of Campston Hill,
northeast of
Llanivangel Crucorney

## Nearest railway

Abergavenny

## Refreshments

Hen & Chickens PH 🍴, plenty of choice in **Abergavenny**
(Clytha Arms PH 🍴🍴, west of **Raglan**, instruction 8)
Ship PH 🍴, plenty of choice in **Raglan**
Hostry Inn, **Llantilio Crossenny**
Three Salmons PH, near **Cross Ash**
Skirrid Inn 🍴🍴, **Llanivangel Crucorney**
Crown PH, **Pantygelli**

## Places of interest

**Abergavenny** *1*
Spectacular mountain ranges surround
this market town on the River Usk. The
labyrinth of narrow streets, some with
Tudor buildings, testifies to the town's
long history, linked to the fortunes of the
ruined 11th-century castle. The castle
now houses a collection of old farming
equipment. The museum in the 19th-
century hunting lodge traces the town's
history

**Raglan Castle** *12*
Romantic ruins of the 15th-century,
moated fortress with a massive hexago-
nal keep, two courtyards and a double-
fronted gatehouse. The surrender of the
castle to Parliamentarians in 1646
marked the end of the Civil War

**White Castle** *14 (2½ km (1½ miles) off the
route)*
Ruined, moated castle on a windswept
hilltop, one of the 'Three Castles of
Gwent' –
a triangle of
fortresses pro-
tecting the border
against the Welsh.
The castle dates
from the 12th century
and was strengthened
by Edward I a century
later

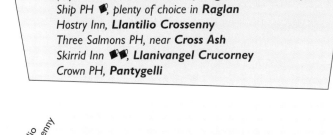

**1** With back to the Baptist church L towards Monmouth and Hereford. After 200 m (yd) 1st R opposite car park. At T-j L 'Museum of Childhood' towards Farmers Arms PH

**2** At X-roads at the end of Lion Street SA onto Lower Monk Street 'B4233 Rockfield 12, Hospital' then immediately L onto Ross Road

**3** At T-j bear R (in effect SA) (NS) then shortly 1st R onto Tredilion Road

**4** Climb. At X-roads by pylons SA past Tredilion Fruit Farm

**5** At T-j (with B4233) L then 1st R. (For short cut, do not take the 1st R but continue SA and rejoin route at Llantilio Crossenny, instruction 14)

**6** At T-j bear L through Llandewi Rhydderch. After 2 km (1¼ miles) at the top of short hill R 'Penpergwm'. Fast descent

**7** After 1 km (¾ mile) as road swings sharp right 1st L (NS)

**8** At T-j near to the bridge over the A40 L then 1st R 'Great Oak 1'

**9** Shortly after telephone box and RH bend in Great Oak 1st L (NS). At T-j by triangle of grass R (NS)

▼ The Skirrid Mountain (Ysgyryd Fawr) near Abergavenny

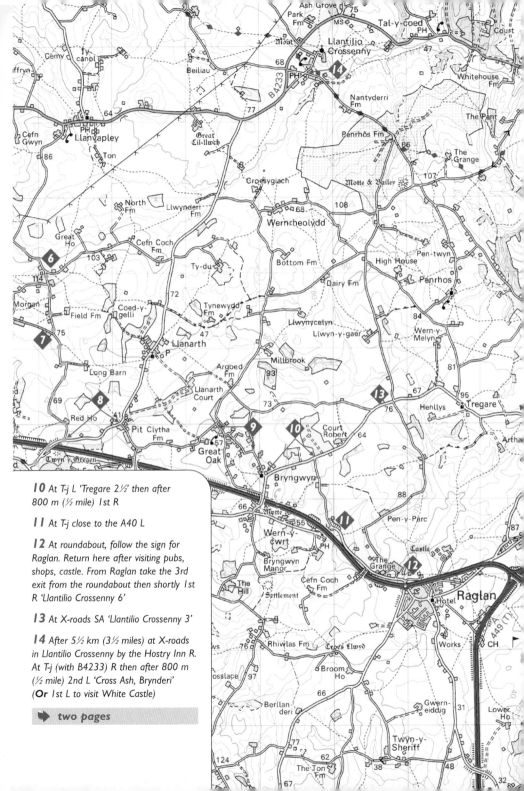

**10** At T-j L 'Tregare 2½' then after 800 m (½ mile) 1st R

**11** At T-j close to the A40 L

**12** At roundabout, follow the sign for Raglan. Return here after visiting pubs, shops, castle. From Raglan take the 3rd exit from the roundabout then shortly 1st R 'Llantilio Crossenny 6'

**13** At X-roads SA 'Llantilio Crossenny 3'

**14** After 5½ km (3½ miles) at X-roads in Llantilio Crossenny by the Hostry Inn R. At T-j (with B4233) R then after 800 m (½ mile) 2nd L 'Cross Ash, Brynderi' (**Or** 1st L to visit White Castle)

➡ two pages

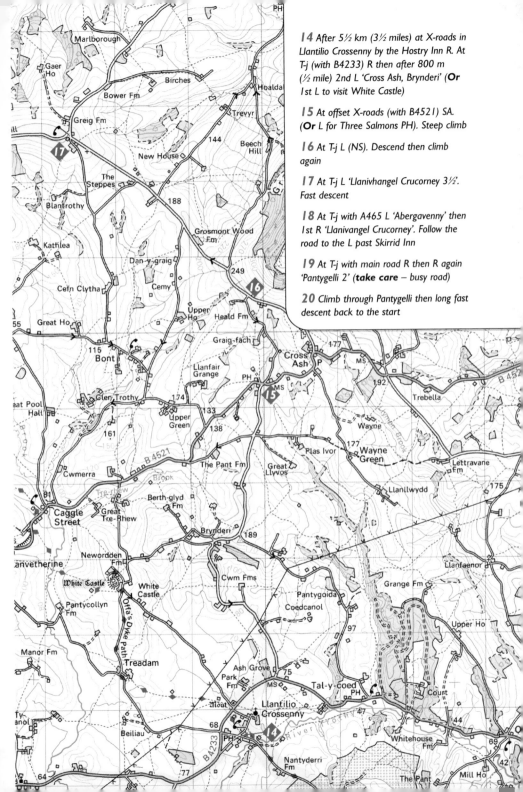

**14** After 5½ km (3½ miles) at X-roads in Llantilio Crossenny by the Hostry Inn R. At T-j (with B4233) R then after 800 m (½ mile) 2nd L 'Cross Ash, Brynderi' (**Or** 1st L to visit White Castle)

**15** At offset X-roads (with B4521) SA. (**Or** L for Three Salmons PH). Steep climb

**16** At T-j L (NS). Descend then climb again

**17** At T-j L 'Llanivhangel Crucorney 3½'. Fast descent

**18** At T-j with A465 L 'Abergavenny' then 1st R 'Llanivangel Crucorney'. Follow the road to the L past Skirrid Inn

**19** At T-j with main road R then R again 'Pantygelli 2' (**take care** – busy road)

**20** Climb through Pantygelli then long fast descent back to the start

# South from Rhayader and back along the Wye Valley

**R**hayader is a fine base for exploring Mid-Wales. The busy A470 to the south should be avoided, but parallel to it and to the west lies the mixture of moorland tracks and wooded lanes that constitute the delights of this ride. The wobbly, suspension footbridge over the Elan River is crossed on the outward and return legs. Southwest of Llanwrthwl you climb steeply up onto the moorland of Rhos Saith-maen where navigation might be difficult for a short section in poor visibility. A mixture of quiet wooded lanes, carrying only a handful of vehicles a day, and fine stone tracks complete the loop as the

ride drops back down to the Wye Valley to the north of Newbridge. The outward route is joined at Llanwrthwl and followed back to the cafes, tea shops and pubs of Rhayader.

## Start

The clocktower at the crossroads in the centre of Rhayader

P Parking by the Leisure Centre and Tourist Information Centre, on the A470 north towards Llangurig

## Distance and grade

32 km (20 miles)

/// Moderate

## Terrain

Wooded river valley, moorland, quiet lanes. Three main climbs: 230 m (760 ft) from Llanwrthwl to the moorland top on Rhos Saith-maen; 150 m (490 ft) from the

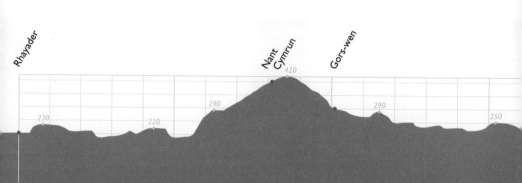

B4358 onto Banc Creigol; 90 m (295 ft) from the Wye at Cefncoed northwest towards Llanwrthwl. Lowest point – 160 m (525 ft) at the River Wye at Cefncoed. Highest point – 420 m (1380 ft) on the moorland of Rhos Saithmaen

## Nearest railway

Llandrindod Wells, 6½ km (4 miles) east of the route

## Places of interest

### Rhayader /
Sheltered on all sides by mountains, this small market town is itself 210 m (700 ft) above sea level and lies on the River Wye. The four main streets form a crossroad and an attractive clock tower crowned by a cross stands in East Street. It was built in 1924 on the site once occupied by an 18th-century Town Hall. Rhayader is Welsh for 'The Cataract on the Wye' and a cataract was there until 1780, when a single span bridge was built. The present arched bridge dates from 1929 and all that remains of the cataract are some modest rapids

### Elan Valley /
Known as the Welsh 'Lake District', the man-made dams and reservoirs to the west are a spectacular attraction. There are five reservoirs – four opened in 1904 and the fifth in 1952, forming 16 km (10 miles) of sweeping lake land from the high moorlands above Craig Goch to the woodlands of Caban Goch

## Refreshments

Plenty of choice in **Rhayader**
Red Lion PH, **Llanafan-fawr**

◀ Footbridge across the Afon Elan south of Rhayader

Hirnant

Llanwrthwl

420

340
300
230
200
190
220
240

20          25          30     32

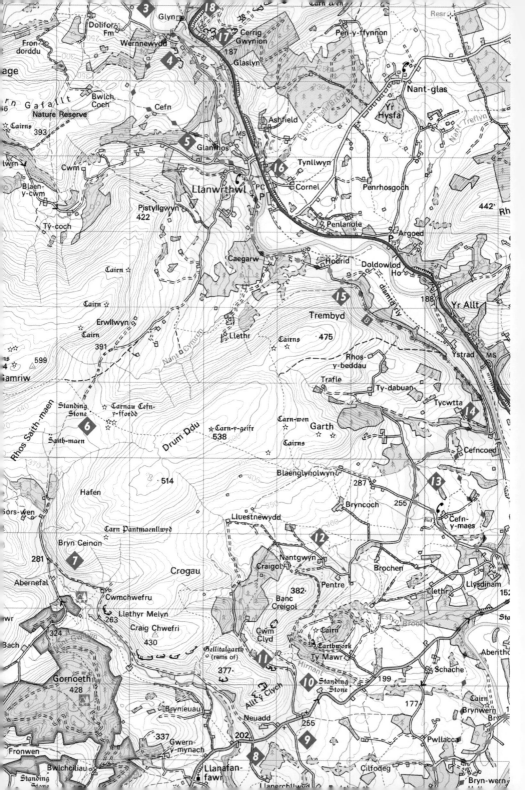

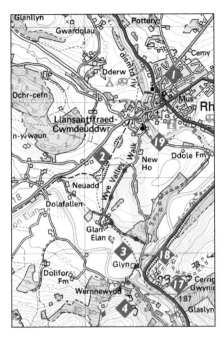

**1** From the clock tower take West Street past the Lion Royal Hotel towards the Elan Valley. Cross the bridge over the river then 1st road L by telephone box 'Unsuitable for HGV's'

**2** Go past New House on your left. Shortly after, on a sharp LH bend leave tarmac and bear R (in effect SA) onto track. Gentle descent. After 1 km (¾ mile) take the 1st track to L 'Bridleway'. Go past buildings. Ignore 1st left at fork, 30 m (yd) further on, just before the old railway bridge, take next L 'Bridleway'

**3** At T-j with road R. At the end of tarmac by a stone barn turn L downhill (yellow arrow) through gate onto track. Cross wobbly bridge over river and turn L (yellow arrow)

**4** At T-j with road L alongside river

**5** At T-j after 2½ km (1½ miles) with 'Elan Village' signposted in both directions turn L downhill, then shortly 1st R onto no through road 'Pen Rhos only'

**6** Climb steeply on tarmac to its end. Continue in same direction on track which becomes grassy once over the brow of the hill. Aim to the right of the conifer plantation ahead. Descend past neat stone cottage

**7** Track turns to tarmac. At fork of lanes bear L. Lovely descent.

**8** At T-j (with B4358) turn L (**Or** turn R for Red Lion PH)

**9** Go past the Pisgah Baptist Chapel on the right. At the brow of the hill L 'Unsuitable for HGVs'

**10** After 1 km (¾ mile), on a LH bend in a dip in the road bear R over cattle grid onto track 'Cwm Clyd Isaf'. After 200 m (yd) of descent, at the end of a LH bend 1st R through field gate onto grassy track

**11** Cross stream. At the end of enclosed track, go through gate on the left then immediately R through second gate and uphill across field towards wood. Steep climb then descent

**12** At T-j with tarmac near to farm, turn sharp R. Go past a farm on the left, then one on the right and follow road round sharp LH bend

**13** At X-roads by 'Give Way' sign SA then after 800 m (½ mile) next R on tarmac lane

**14** At bottom of hill turn sharp L over stone bridge then bear R (in effect SA) onto grassy/stone track. Steady climb then descent

**15** After 3 km (2 miles) where the track turns to tarmac at gate bear L

**16** After 3 km (2 miles) at T-j by the church in Llanwrthwl L 'Elan Village 4½'. At the end of the village fork R 'Elan Village 4¼'. (You have now rejoined outward route). Steep climb then 1st road R 'Elan Village 4¼, Rhayader 3¼'

**17** After 2½ km (1½ miles) on a sharp LH bend as the road swings steeply uphill, bear R (in effect SA) onto track 'Wye Valley Walk' (blue horse sign)

**18** Cross wobbly bridge, bear R across field. Exit field by farm, turn R and follow the lane back to Rhayader

**19** At T-j with B4518 R to return to the clocktower

# *Moorland tracks north of New Radnor*

Close to the border of England, to the east of Builth Wells lies a veritable feast of fine bridleways and byways, criss-crossing not only the dramatic upland of Radnor Forest but also the hills around Glascwm to the south of the A44 and the hills to the north of the A488 between the valleys of the Rivers Ithon and Teme. The hills of Radnor Forest, explored in this ride, rise to over 610 m (2000 ft). As they are set apart from the main north-south line of the Cambrian Mountains, running up through the centre of Wales, the views are spectacular, particularly those on the second half of the ride looking from the eastern flanks of Bache Hill down into the River Lugg Valley and across to England. The ride climbs to over 520 m (1700 ft) on both the outward and return legs of the trip. If you enjoy this ride, there are plenty more legally rideable tracks in the area that might tempt you to devise your own route.

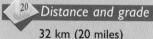

### Start

The Eagle Hotel, New Radnor, on the A44, 21 km (13 miles) northeast of Builth Wells

P No specific car park – show consideration

### Distance and grade

32 km (20 miles)

///// Strenuous

### Terrain

Farmland, high moorland, forestry. Two climbs of just over 300 m (1000 ft), one near the beginning and one after halfway. Three other climbs of 61–91 m (200–300 ft) between the two

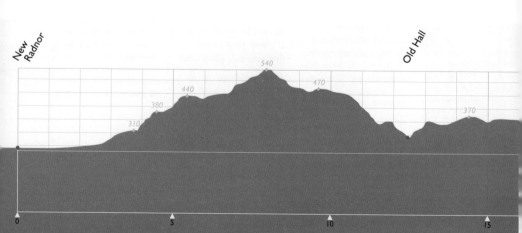

major climbs. Lowest point – 230 m (755 ft) near Bleddfa. Highest points – 540 m (1790 ft) on the moorland on the western side of the route, 530 m (1740 ft) on the moorland on the eastern side of the route

### Nearest railway

Dolau is 3 km (2 miles) west of the route

### Places of interest

#### New Radnor 1
Almost 1000 years of turbulent history lie behind New Radnor, new at the time of Edward the Confessor. It was founded by Earl Harold Godwinsson in 1064 as a stronghold commanding a valley leading from the English border into Wales. The Earl became King Harold, only to be killed at the Battle of Hastings in 1066. The Normans laid out New Radnor on a neat, gridiron pattern, best seen from the steep, grassy mound, which is all that remains of the Norman castle keep. New Radnor's last battle was fought in 1644 when it fell to Cromwell's troops after a brief siege

#### The Whimble 20
Once famous for its summer harvest of whinberries used for dyeing Lancashire's cotton

### Refreshments

Eagle Hotel (also serves tea), Radnor Arms PH, **New Radnor** Hundred House PH 🍺, **Bleddfa**

▲ Looking north over the River Lugg valley from Ednol Hill

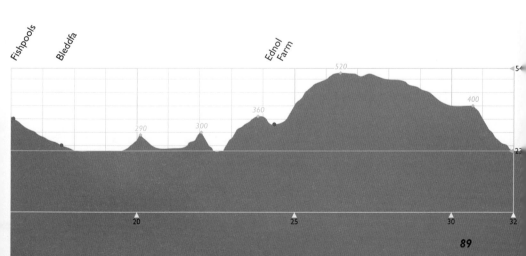

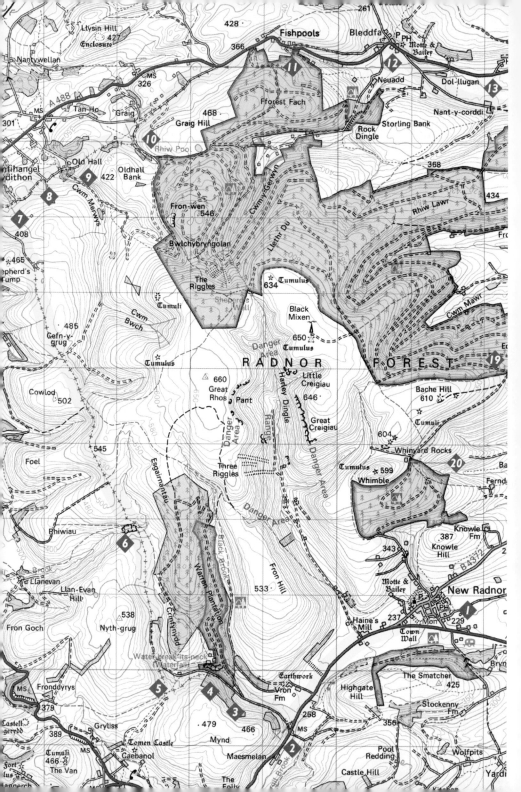

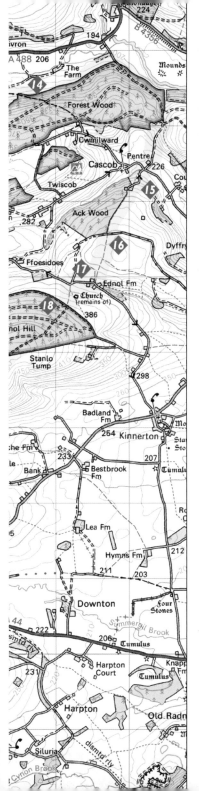

**1** With back to the Eagle Hotel in New Radnor R uphill then follow road L 'Rhayader 19'. At T-j with A44 R

**2** After 2½ km (1½ miles), at the base of the conical hill and immediately after a tarmac turning to the left, turn sharply R uphill onto track

**3** At fork of tracks after 1 km (¾ mile) bear L (red arrow)

**4** At second fork bear R. Go through gate and past metal barn

**5** At third fork bear L through gate (red arrow). Follow rough track over open moorland

**6** The rough section improves after crossing a stream on a LH bend. On the descent follow the red arrows on wooden marker posts. The track turns to tarmac at barn

**7 Easy to miss.** On fast road descent, shortly after a sharp RH bend turn R over cattle grid onto good stone track 'Pen Rochell'

**8** Ignore left turn to Rochell. At T-j of tracks with a round, forested hill ahead turn R towards then through gate. Bear L

**9** At X-roads of tracks by pond and farm buildings SA. Follow along LH edge of conifer plantation

**10** At T-j with broad track bear L (in effect SA). Shortly, at junction of several tracks at the bottom of a dip, with a tarmac lane to the left, turn R uphill on broad stone track

**11** At T-j with main road (A488) R. Climb to the brow of the hill. **Easy to miss.** On the descent, shortly after a RH bend with chevrons bear 1st L uphill onto wide gravel track towards cottage

**12** Track turns to tarmac. At T-j with A488 L. 200 m (yd) after passing the Hundred House Inn take the 1st road R. Ignore turnings to left and right

**13** At the end of the tarmac go SA through farm, start climb then 1st R through gate onto enclosed track. Steep push

**14** At T-j with forestry track bear L. At offset X-roads with wider forestry track L gently downhill. Descend then climb. Exit forestry. Superb descent

**15** At X-roads with road L then R. Tarmac turns to track at farm

**16** At grassy X-roads at edge of plantation SA. The last section of the downhill may be overgrown

**17** At T-j with road R then 1st track L opposite drive to New House Farm. After 150 m (yd) go through the RH of the gates and uphill along LH field edge (may be rough)

**18** Through bridle gate and diagonally L uphill on steep track through forestry plantation. At X-roads of tracks SA. Ignore a left then a right turn

**19** At fork of tracks at the edge of the forestry bear L to exit woodland. Magnificent views to the left

**20** Enter forestry and follow track down through woodland. Exit via gate and descend steeply on tarmac. At T-j at the end of Mutton Dingle R then L to return to start

# 3 *Tracks over heather-clad hills around Glascwm*

*T*he second of the two rides that explore the magnificent network of tracks south of Newtown and north of Hay-on-Wye covering the hills lying between the A470/A483 and the Wales/England border. The tracks tend to be well drained and maintained and relatively easy to follow over the steep, heather-clad moorland that rises to almost 550 m (1800 ft). The views are frequently spectacular, none more so than those that reward you at the top of the first steep climb from the start at Hundred House up to the tumulus at the Giants Grave. For the lover of exhilarating cycling on open hills, the descent is a dream come true, crossing the moorland and following tracks between stone walls down to the church at Glascwm. The second hill follows a similar pattern, a steep climb of 240 m (800 ft) leads on to a fast descent. The first two climbs are the hardest, and with the exception of a short, steep push southwest from the A481, the going in the second half of the ride is much more undulating with more gradual climbs and descents past isolated farmsteads and through the fern and heather of these lovely hills.

## Start

The Hundred House Inn on the A481, 8 km (5 miles) to the east of Builth Wells

P Car park on the green uphill from the PH

## 20 Distance and grade

34 km (21 miles)

///// Strenuous

## Terrain

Fine tracks over heather- and fern-clad hills. Four main climbs: 241 m (790 ft) from the start to Giants Grave; 240 m (800 ft)

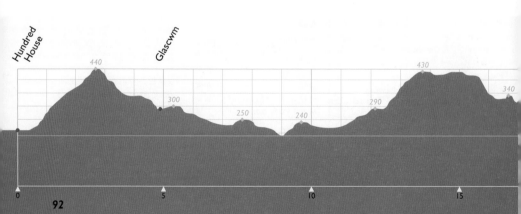

from Cregrina to Doctor's Pool; 130 m (430 ft) from the farm at Harbour to Black Yatt; 61 m (200 ft) from the A481 onto Bryn y Maen. Highest point – 440 m (1450 ft) at the Giants Grave tumulus. Lowest point – 190 m (610 ft) at the River Edw at Cregrina

## Nearest railway

Builth Road, 10 km (6 miles) west of the start

## Places of interest

**Aberedw** 1 *(just west off the route)*
The tiny village, 5 km (3 miles) southeast of Builth Wells, nestles in a steep wooded valley with the impressive limestone crags of Aberedw Rocks rising to more than 300 m (1000 ft) above the south bank of the River Edw. Among the rocks is a small cave where Llywelyn ap Gruffydd, last of the original Princes of Wales, is said to have hidden shortly before being killed by English soldiers in 1282

▼ *Into the hills above Hundred House*

## Refreshments

Hundred House Inn 🍺, **Hundred House**

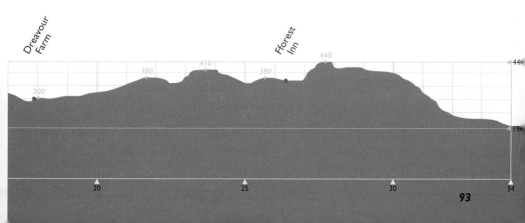

**1** With back to the Hundred House Inn turn L along the A481 towards New Radnor. Cross stream, climb for 400 m (¼ mile) then turn R onto no through road 'Rhiw Farm'. Steep climb

**2** Tarmac turns to stone track then grassy track up past the tumulus of the Giants Grave. Superb views. Fine descent on magnificent grass track, soon enclosed by walls

**3** At fork of tracks at start of pronounced stream valley bear L. Track turns to tarmac

**4** At T-j by telephone box and Youth Hostel in Glascwm R.

**5** After 2½ km (1½ miles) which includes a descent then short climb, on a sharp RH bend take the 1st road L 'Cregrina 1'. At T-j at the bottom of hill L 'Aberedw 5½'. Steep climb. Go over brow of hill, descend for 400 m (¼ mile) ignoring 1st left (track to farm)

**6** Take next road L 'Rhulen ¾'

**7** After 2 km (1¼ miles) fork L onto no through road. Tarmac turns to track. Steep push

**8** At X-roads of tracks at top of hill SA. Magnificent views

**9** At T-j with tarmac on hairpin bend bear L downhill. As the track swings sharp left uphill bear R (in effect SA) to cross stream

**10** At T-j shortly after farm L. At next T-j L 'Glascwm 1½'

**11** At X-roads SA onto no through road

**12** Tarmac turns to track. Go past one farm on left. At the second house (Cwm Kesty), as the stone track swings sharp L, go SA onto grassy track, through gate entrance ahead and along LH edge of field. This joins a better track at the next gate. Grassy track past small pond

**13** **Easy to miss.** After gentle downhill, at junction where track bends right then left uphill towards hills turn L downhill alongside fence. At next junction of tracks just past a second pond turn L alongside

row of trees on a level path. Track turns to tarmac at Foice Farm

**14** At T-j with A44 L then 1st L onto track by lake. Through gate and turn R through second gate on steep grassy track. Fantastic views

**15** Descend to the R of tumulus to junction of tracks. Take the RH of the

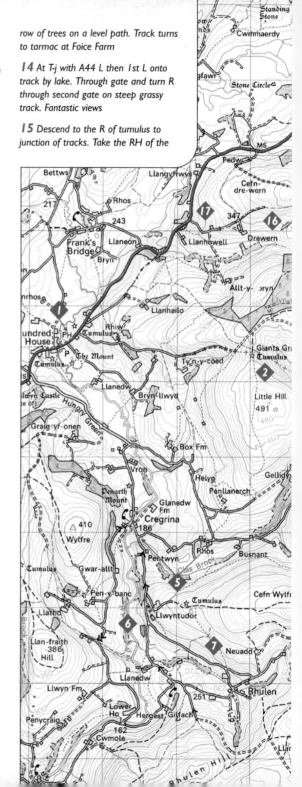

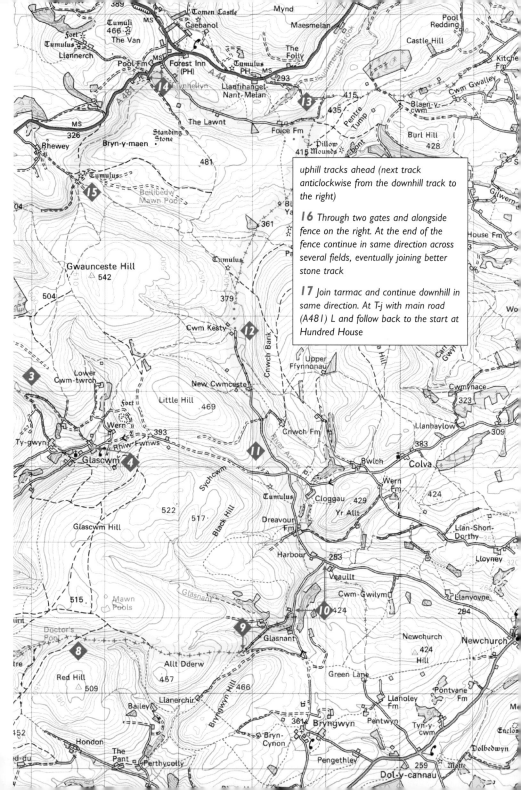

uphill tracks ahead (next track anticlockwise from the downhill track to the right)

**16** Through two gates and alongside fence on the right. At the end of the fence continue in same direction across several fields, eventually joining better stone track

**17** Join tarmac and continue downhill in same direction. At T-j with main road (A481) L and follow back to the start at Hundred House

# Along the Llyn Brianne Reservoir and west over moorland tracks

**Start**

The RSPB/Dinas car park 13 km (8 miles) north of Llandovery and 5½ km (3½ miles) north of Rhandirmwyn, on the road running along the east side of the River Tywi. The car park is on the left

P As above

**Distance and grade**

32 km (20 miles)

Strenuous

**W**ith stretches of deciduous woodlands along its hillsides, the Tywi Valley is one of the most beautiful in Wales; the Llyn Brianne Reservoir, which captures its water, adds to its loveliness. The track around the reservoir is followed for several kilometres, and if the clouds are low it would be worthwhile considering a complete circuit of the reservoir as an alternative to the route described. From the valley of the Camddwr at the northern end of the reservoir the route climbs steeply on a rough and challenging track up onto the top of the moorland. A steep grassy descent links to the track past the youth hostel and a section on moorland lanes before the final steep climb of the day on the unexpected broad stone track across the moorland. The descent and the valley of the Pysgotwr is breathtaking in its beauty. One realises how much more attractive broadleaf woodlands are than the ubiquitous conifer plantations of the area. This delightful valley is followed to its junction with the Tywi and the start is soon reached after rejoining the road north from Rhandirmwyn.

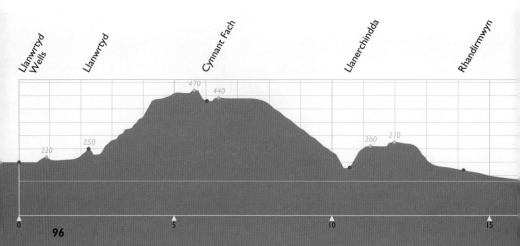

## Terrain

Reservoir, forestry, high moorland. Five climbs – 100 m (330 ft) from the start to the reservoir; 120 m (400 ft) from the reservoir into the forestry to the west of Llyn Brianne; 140 m (460 ft) from the river valley north of the reservoir to the high moorland plateau; 450 m (480 ft) up past the youth hostel onto tarmac; 130 m (430 ft) on the bridleway over the moorland. Lowest point – 140 m (460 ft) at the crossing of the River Tywi near the end of the ride. Highest point – 440 m (1460 ft) on the old road over the moorland to the northwest of the reservoir

## Nearest railway

Llanwrtyd Wells and Llandovery are both 19 km (12 miles) from the route

## Places of interest

### Doethie Valley 8

The Doethie flows down a remote valley before joining another mountain river, the Pysgotwr, and then the larger River Tywi. Near the confluence lies the Wales' equivalent to the secret glades of Sherwood Forest. High in the wooded hills above the watery junction is the cave in which Twm Shon Catti sought refuge from the Sheriff of Camarthen in the 16th century. Twm, or Thomas Jones, described in conflicting reports as both a *bona fide* villain and a local hero, hid from the sheriff in a cave well concealed among the jumble of giant rocks on the distinctive, conical-shaped Dinas Hill

## Refreshments

Towy Bridge Inn, Royal Oak PH, **Rhandirmwyn** (both are south of the start/finish)

Llanwrtyd

510
480
340
250
220
190
150

20      25      30    32

**1** Turn L out of the RSPB car park on the road north from Rhamdirmwyn towards the Lyn Brianne Reservoir

**2** After 2 km (1¼ miles) take the second road to the L, just before the cattle grid. Cross the dam and follow the main track around the edge of the reservoir for 5½ km (3½ mile) crossing a major stream and climbing steadily

**3** As the views open up ahead of a large clearing bear L then shortly fork R on the lower track towards the clearing

**4** At the bottom of a long descent over 3 km (2 miles) at a junction of several tracks by a large white stone house and a small stone barn (near to the road) turn L steeply uphill on a rough stone track (**not** the broad smooth track just beyond it). Very steep push at the start

**5** Once at the top, some sections are likely to be rough/muddy at almost all times of the year. Steep descent

**6** Cross the ford and start climbing again. Climb past the Youth Hostel. Track turns to tarmac. Cross stream

**7** Just before the forestry starts on the left take the first road L

**8** Go past farm and onto obvious track climbing steeply over moorland. Unusually good surface for high, moorland track

**9** Steeply downhill into beautiful oak woodland valley. Go past farm and cross river. At second farm bear R

**10** Follow lovely lane alongside river. At T-j by triangle of grass L 'Llyn Brianne' to return to the start

▼ Llyn Brianne Reservoir

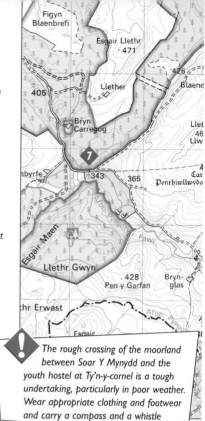

The rough crossing of the moorland between Soar Y Mynydd and the youth hostel at Ty'n-y-cornel is a tough undertaking, particularly in poor weather. Wear appropriate clothing and footwear and carry a compass and a whistle

# 5 Valleys and forest tracks west of Llanwrtyd Wells

Llanwrtyd Wells and the Neuadd Arms have had a connection with mountain biking from the earliest days of the sport and the town was the location of the man v horse v bike races that were only ever once won by a cyclist. Many routes are possible with the town as a base using the network of forestry roads and bridleways that radiate in all directions. The ride starts gently taking the Abergwesyn road out of town along the valley of the River Irfon. After a short descent to cross one of the tributary streams, there is a sustained climb through the Cwm Henog Forest of over 3 km (2 miles). A fast and at times steep descent to the road at Llanerchindda is followed by one of the steepest road climbs in the area. Magnificent views open up to the north before dropping down to Rhandirmwyn and the only pub en route.

## Start

The Neuadd Arms, Llanwrtyd Wells

P No specific car park

## Distance and grade

32 km (20 miles)

Strenuous

## Terrain

Forestry, river valley. Three main climbs – 250 m (820 ft) from the start to the high point in the forest on the outward leg; 100 m (330 ft) road climb shortly after exit from forest; 370 m (1220 ft) from the Tywi Valley to the highest point of the ride in the forest. Lowest point – 140 m (460 ft) in the Tywi Valley north of Rhandirmwyn. Highest point – 520 m (1700 ft) at the top of the major climb after re-entering the forest

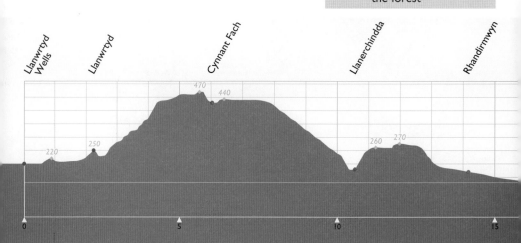

**Nearest railway**

Llanwrtyd Wells

**Refreshments**

Plenty of choice in **Llanwrtyd Wells**
Royal Oak PH 🍴, **Rhandirmwyn**

Towards the top of the on-road climb, the Llyn Brianne Reservoir is well worth a diversion. Leaving the tarmac, there is a steep climb up through the forestry to the high point of the ride. You will need to take care not to miss the turning that links with the outward leg and the fast-track descent back to the Irfon Valley and Llanwrtyd Wells.

▼ The Tywi Valley

The two sections through the forest can be very confusing. Follow the directions carefully, carry a compass with you and check regularly that you are heading in the correct direction

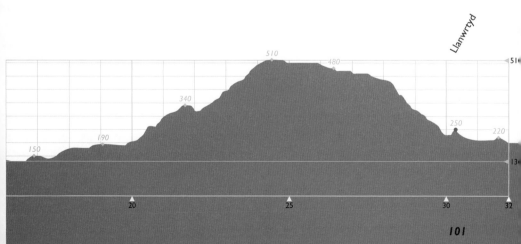

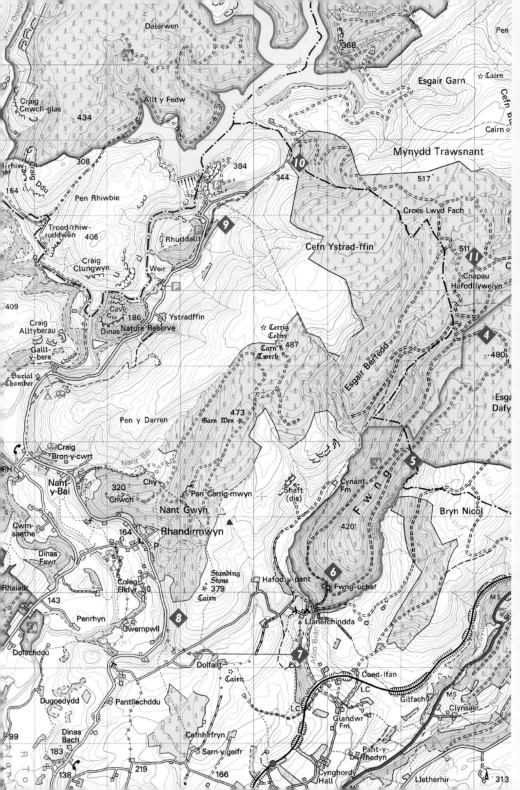

**1** With back to the Neuadd Arms Hotel R out of town 'Abergwesyn 5, Tregaron 17½'

**2** After 2½ km (1½ miles) cross bridge, take the 1st road L just before the church and follow this steeply uphill

**3** At the end of the tarmac by house and buildings bear L downhill on narrow track (blue horse/bridleway sign). Cross stream, climb steeply. At T-j with major forestry track L. Steady climb for 2½ km (1½ miles)

**4** **Ignore** the 1st right turn. At fork after further 1 km bear L downhill. (Try your best to remember this fork – have a good look around you – it is where the outward and return legs join up and it is easily missed on the return). Cross stream and take 1st R by a yellow barrier

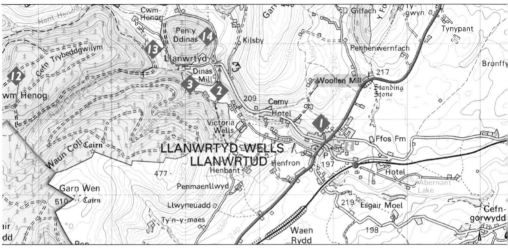

**5** At T-j after 2 km (1¼ miles) R downhill

**6** **Easy to miss.** After fine descent of further 2½ km (1½ miles) turn R down towards house in the woods. At the bottom of a very steep descent R then at T-j with road R again. Cross stream. Very steep on-road climb

**7** The gradient eases. **Easy to miss.** Go past turning to youth hostel on your right. Where the telegraph poles cross from one side to the other, shortly after magnificent views open up ahead and to the right, bear R downhill through metal gate onto track (NS)

**8** Steep descent through woodland (muddy sections). At T-j with road R. Go past the Royal Oak PH, Rhandirmwyn

**9** 7 km (4½ miles) after the pub and 2 km (1¼ miles) after the RSPB car park, it is worth exploring both the roads to the L. The first takes you to a viewpoint of the great spout of water at the bottom of the dam. The second (just before the cattle grid) leads to the top of the dam with fine views of the Llyn Brianne Reservoir

**10** Climb up over the brow of the hill, descend, cross cattle grid and take 1st track R into the forest. Cross earth humps, then at T-j R. Steep 2½ km (1½ mile) climb

**11** **Easy to miss.** Once you have reached the top, in the next 2 km (1¼ miles) you should ignore a left turn (rough/grassy) on a RH bend, ignore in quick succession a left turn then tracks

to left and right at X-roads (all of them rough/grassy). On a downhill RH hairpin bend turn L onto level track to rejoin outward route. (If you get to a yellow metal barrier you have gone too far)

**12** At fork bear R (blue arrow on yellow square). Superb descent

**13** Shortly after exiting forestry via wooden bridle gate adjacent to field gate take the next track R (blue arrow).

**14** Cross stream, climb on narrow track. At T-j at the end of narrow track R past farm on tarmac lane. At the T-j by the church R and follow this lane back to the start

# 6 *Moorland and forestry tracks east of Llandovery*

On many of the best, off-road routes in Wales you have two dilemmas to resolve: the first is that the best views are from the tops of the hills, but the higher you go the more likely that the bridleways over moorland will be vague and boggy; the second is that many of the best, year-round tracks are in land owned by the Forestry Commission and the network of forest roads is constantly being enlarged for forestry operations. As these additional tracks take time to find their way onto maps, getting lost is a probability rather than a possibility. With these two dilemmas in mind, this ride aims, as much as possible, to gain height on good tracks on the southern half of the ride and to keep the route through forestry simple on the northern half of the ride. Starts from the valley of the River Gwydderig and climb steeply to the course of the old Roman road that used to run between Trecastle and Llandovery. After a ridge

## Start

The car park/lay-by 8 km (5 miles) to the east of Llandovery on the A40, just east of the scattered houses at Halfway

P As above

## Distance and grade

38 km (24 miles)

//////  Strenuous

## Terrain

River valley, moorland and forestry tracks. Three tough climbs – 280 m (920 ft) from the start to the top of Mynydd Myddfai; 120 m (400 ft) from the bottom of the valley near Myddfai to the top of the hill above the A40; 220 m (730 ft) after crossing the A40 to the high point in Crychan Forest. Lowest point – 91 m (300 ft) at the

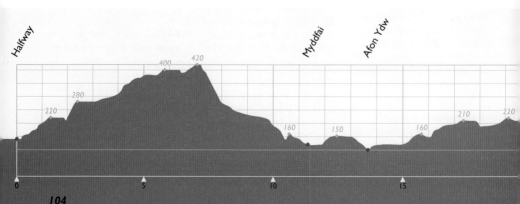

crossing of the River Gwyderrig halfway round the ride. Highest point – 420 m (1380 ft) at the southernmost point of the ride on Mynydd Myddfai

### Nearest railway

Llandovery, 5 km (3 miles) west of the route at the western crossing of the A40

### Refreshments

Plough Inn, **Myddfai**

section with magnificent views, the route drops down to Myddfai, with the only pub on the ride. A circuitous route via woodland and old county roads leads back down into the Gwyderrig Valley with the distinctive lump of Mwmffri looming ahead. The roller coaster ride climbs through forestry, descends, and then climbs for a final time before the great downhill rush back to the start.

### Places of interest

**Y Pigwyn 3**
Roman legions marched along the high track between Trecastle and Llandovery in about AD 50. There is evidence of their camps at points as high as 411 m (yd)

▼ The decent towards Myddfai

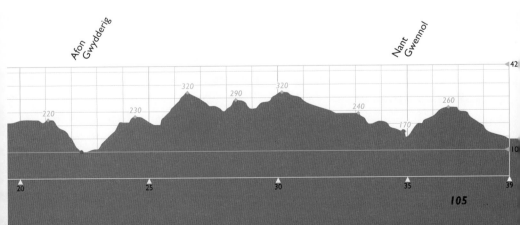

**1** From the car park turn L along the A40 towards Llandovery. After 400 m (¼ mile) take the 1st road L. Steep climb. Go through gate. Cross two small streams at the bottom of short descents. The second is followed by very steep climb

**2** At T-j L onto no through road. Tarmac turns to track at the farm. Ignore the bridleway to the right soon after the farm. Climb steeply on broad stone track

**3** Shortly after passing the top of a stream valley to the left turn R by a wooden post onto grassy track. At two forks bear R. Continue southwest then west climbing towards the hilltop then follow track as it bears R. The track starts descending, the gradient steepens

**4** Where the track appears to run out turn sharp R (north) along the line of reeds. The track surface improves and goes past farm

**5** At T-j by Pen-twyn L

**6** At T-j in Myddfai L then R by Plough Inn following the road round to the R past the church-yard

**7** Steep descent, cross bridge over river and immediately R sharply back on yourself onto track. After 400 m (¼ mile) fork R

**8** Go through several metal gates and past delightful round house called 'Round Lodge'. At X-roads of tracks by double gates turn R uphill 'Dyfed CC. Right of Way'. Muddy section

**9** At X-roads with road and a house to the left SA

**10** At X-roads with next road R steeply uphill

**11** After 1 km (¾ mile) (and shortly after passing the farm of Cefntelych on the right) take the 1st road to the L

**12** After 600 m (yd) go past farm on left. After futher 600 m (yd) turn R on stone track. At X-roads of tracks SA. Continue SA through several gates. This becomes a fast forestry track. **Take care** on the descent as the track ends at the busy A40

**13** At X-roads with main road SA onto minor road 'Pentre-ty-gwyn 1, Babel 2'. Follow the road round to the L after crossing bridge. After 800 m (½ mile) 1st road L

**14** After 2½ km (1½ miles), at X-roads of tracks at the end of the tarmac SA uphill on steep stony track. Through gate and along RH edge of field

**15** Follow the track as it swings in a wide arc uphill and round to the L towards the corner of the forest. Enter the forest and at fork bear L gently downhill

**16** Go round two sweeping LH bends on gentle descent. Start climbing. At T-j on hairpin bend bear L downhill

**17** Shortly, at major junction of several tracks, go SA onto the track that swings L then R uphill. At T-j with a large clearing to the right turn R gently downhill

**18** At a 5-way junction with the gate of Cwm Coed Eco Lodge to the right take the LH of the uphill tracks ahead of you (it is the less steep of the two). Climb with fine views to the left

**19** **Ignore** three turns to the right on the descent. At X-roads of tracks just before the main track starts climbing again turn R then fork R. Keep bearing L, ignoring right turns

> **!** The section through the forest can be very confusing. Follow the directions carefully, carry a compass with you and check regularly that you are heading in the correct direction

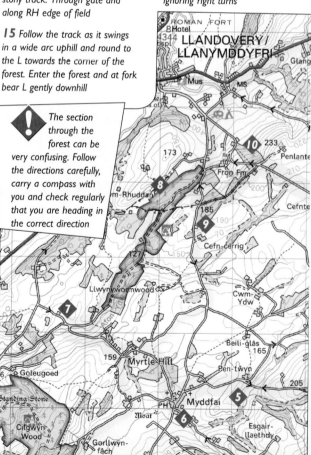

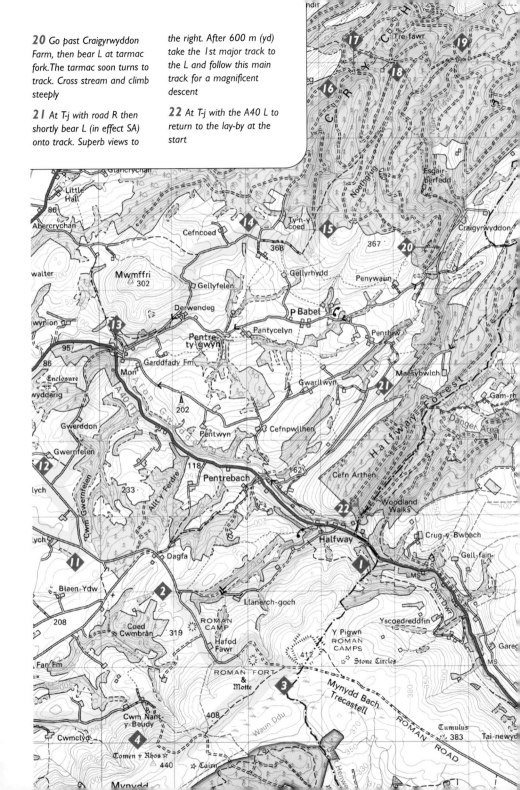

**20** Go past Craigyrwyddon Farm, then bear L at tarmac fork. The tarmac soon turns to track. Cross stream and climb steeply

**21** At T-j with road R then shortly bear L (in effect SA) onto track. Superb views to

the right. After 600 m (yd) take the 1st major track to the L and follow this main track for a magnificent descent

**22** At T-j with the A40 L to return to the lay-by at the start

# *Reservoirs and mountain passes south of Brecon*

Starting north of Merthyr Tydfil from the Garwnant Forest Centre, this very long off-road ride heads north through the forestry before dropping down to the busy A470. After this unavoidable stretch, a fine off-road descent is followed by a delightful section of lanes beneath the towering slopes of Pen y Fan, Corn Du and Cribyn. The major climb of the day, largely on a stony track, which will involve some pushing, is rewarded with views of the mountains ahead. A long descent leads to the dismantled railway that is followed off and on for almost 13 km (8 miles) to the northern edge of Merthyr Tydfil. The Taf Fawr Valley is followed back north steeply through forestry and then alongside the Llwyn-on Reservoir back to the start.

 Start

Garwnant Forest Centre, at the northern end of the Llwyn-on Reservoir on the A470, 8 km (5 miles) north of Merthyr Tydfil

P As above

➡️ **two pages**

**4** At T-j with A470 L 'Brecon'. Gentle climb for 3 km (2 miles) on busy A470

**5** Immediately after the forest ends on the right (opposite car parking area to the left) bear R by telephone box onto track 'Brecon. Taff Trail'. Gently descending track turns to tarmac at Blaenglyn

**6** Shortly after road junction sign, just before stone house turn R on tarmac lane

**7** At T-j with broader lane bear R 'Taff Trail'. After 1 km (¾ mile) 1st R at X-roads. Shortly, at next X-roads SA to cross bridge

**8** After 1 km (¾ mile) 1st R opposite MOD signpost. **Ignore** right turn by cattle grid, follow road round to the L then shortly take the next road R over bridge

**9** At T-j after 2 km (1¼ miles) R. At T-j after 1 km (¾ mile) R downhill to cross stream. Long climb, at times steep, on tarmac then track

**10** Follow main stone track alongside the wall to the L. Superb views open up. Go over the pass

**11** Long fine descent, with one steep gully to navigate, then a short rough/muddy section. At T-j with road L then L again onto track

➡️ **two pages**

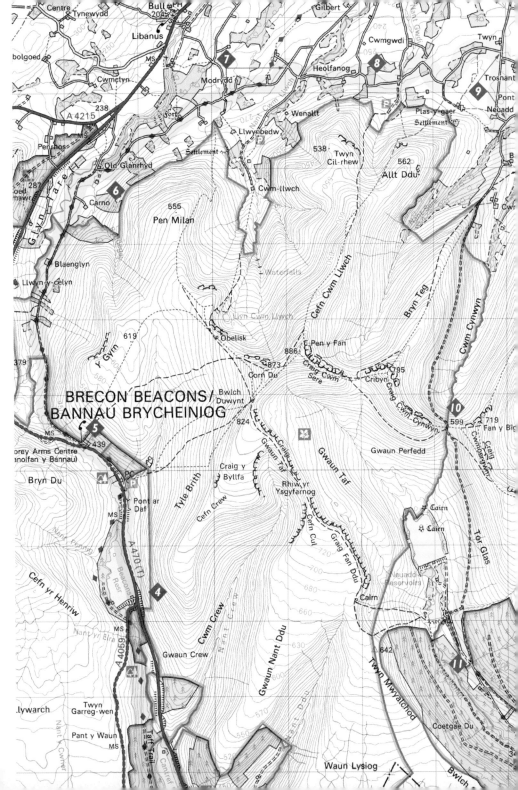

**1** From the Visitor Centre go downhill back towards road then take the 1st track on the R sharply back on yourself through green barrier 'Willow Walk' (the 'No cycling' sign refers to the walk by the river, **not** the forestry track)

**2** Climb for 300 m (yd) then 1st R to continue uphill. Follow track for 3 km (2 miles). Go over the brow of the hill, ignoring bridleway signs to left and right

**3** Shortly after a RH bend, opposite Taff Trail signpost, bear L uphill on rough track. Exit forestry over a stile, push your bike across 150 m (yd) of rough moorland. At T-j with road (A4059) R

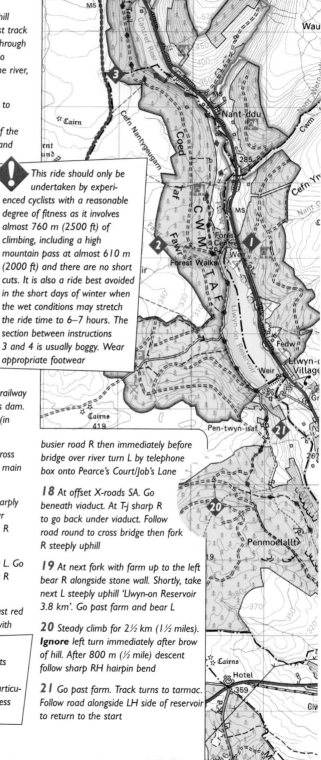

! This ride should only be undertaken by experienced cyclists with a reasonable degree of fitness as it involves almost 760 m (2500 ft) of climbing, including a high mountain pass at almost 610 m (2000 ft) and there are no short cuts. It is also a ride best avoided in the short days of winter when the wet conditions may stretch the ride time to 6–7 hours. The section between instructions 3 and 4 is usually boggy. Wear appropriate footwear

◀ **two pages**

**12** At T-j with road, diagonally R onto tarmac which becomes track and follows course of dismantled railway

**13** At the buildings of Dolygaer Mountain Centre after 3 km (2 miles) turn R off the railway path then at T-j with road R to cross dam. At T-j with more major road bear L (in effect SA) then 1st R into forestry

**14** At T-j in forestry R 'Taff Trail'. Cross wooden bridge over river and follow main track

**15** At T-j with road R then 1st L sharply back on yourself 'Dowlais 3, Merthyr Tydfil 4'. Cross dam bridge and turn R 'Taff Trail'

**16** After 5 km (3 miles) at T-j bear L. Go beneath railway bridge, take the 1st R 'Taff Trail, Merthyr Tydfil'

**17** At the end of trail, take road past red brick and grey stone chapel. At T-j with busier road R then immediately before bridge over river turn L by telephone box onto Pearce's Court/Job's Lane

**18** At offset X-roads SA. Go beneath viaduct. At T-j sharp R to go back under viaduct. Follow road round to cross bridge then fork R steeply uphill

**19** At next fork with farm up to the left bear R alongside stone wall. Shortly, take next L steeply uphill 'Llwyn-on Reservoir 3.8 km'. Go past farm and bear L

**20** Steady climb for 2½ km (1½ miles). **Ignore** left turn immediately after brow of hill. After 800 m (½ mile) descent follow sharp RH hairpin bend

**21** Go past farm. Track turns to tarmac. Follow road alongside LH side of reservoir to return to the start

! The Taff Trail and the Brecon Beacons are popular with cyclists and walkers alike. Please show consideration and common sense, particularly on the descents. The trails are less busy during the week

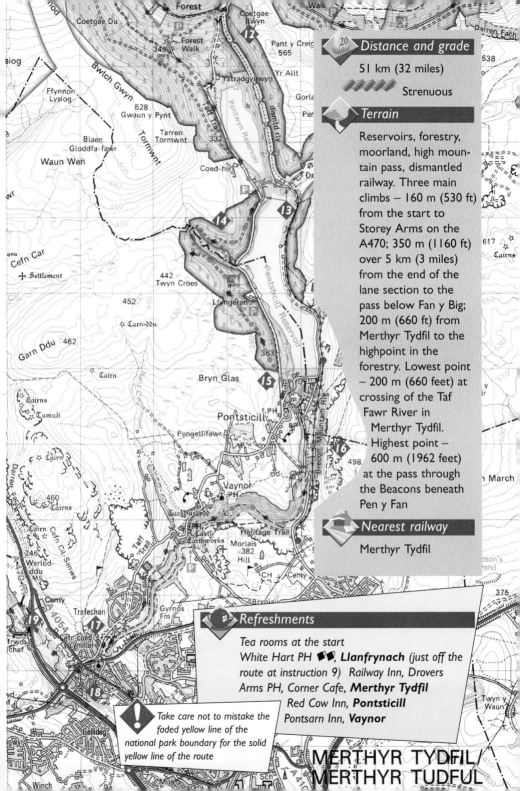

**Distance and grade**

20

**Distance and grade**

51 km (32 miles)

///// Strenuous

**Terrain**

Reservoirs, forestry, moorland, high mountain pass, dismantled railway. Three main climbs – 160 m (530 ft) from the start to Storey Arms on the A470; 350 m (1160 ft) over 5 km (3 miles) from the end of the lane section to the pass below Fan y Big; 200 m (660 ft) from Merthyr Tydfil to the highpoint in the forestry. Lowest point – 200 m (660 feet) at crossing of the Taf Fawr River in Merthyr Tydfil. Highest point – 600 m (1962 feet) at the pass through the Beacons beneath Pen y Fan

**Nearest railway**

Merthyr Tydfil

**Refreshments**

Tea rooms at the start
White Hart PH ♦♦, *Llanfrynach (just off the route at instruction 9)* Railway Inn, Drovers Arms PH, Corner Cafe, **Merthyr Tydfil** Red Cow Inn, **Pontsticill** Pontsarn Inn, **Vaynor**

! Take care not to mistake the faded yellow line of the national park boundary for the solid yellow line of the route

**MERTHYR TYDFIL/**
**MERTHYR TUDFUL**

# 8 From Talybont-on-Usk, the Taff Trail and Brecon Beacons

 Start

The White Hart PH,
Talybont-on-Usk,
10 km (6 miles)
southeast of Brecon

P No specific car
park. Space on the
B4558 between the
pubs and the Post
Office

20 Distance and grade

30 km (19 miles)

Moderate/strenuous

The Taff Trail runs from Cardiff to Brecon and will be part of a trans-Wales route linking Cardiff with Caernarfon. Using dismantled railways, forestry tracks and quiet minor lanes the Taff Trail threads its way through the old industrial heartland of South Wales to the lovely countryside of the Brecon Beacons. A section of the trail is used at the start of a long climb from the canal at Talybont-on-Usk alongside the reservoir. The climb continues through Talybont-on-Usk and Taf Fechan Forests and up the stone track that

> ! The Taff Trail and the Brecon Beacons are popular with cyclists and walkers alike. Please show consideration and common sense, particularly on the descents. The trails are less busy during the week

leads to the pass beneath the high Brecon Beacons ridge. The pass is almost at 610 m (2000 ft) and the views on a fine day are truly spectacular. The descent requires some care on the first stages where the track is steep with loose stones. The gradient eases and the surface improves, turning to a fast, tarmac descent. There is the opportunity of a fine pub stop in Llanfrynach before the last road stretch back to the start.

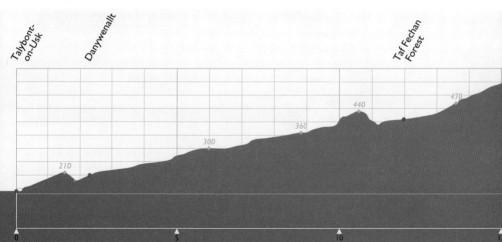

River valley, forestry, high mountain pass. Only one major climb of 470 m (1560 ft) over almost 16 km (10 miles). Lowest point – 120 m (400 ft) at Talybont-on-Usk. Highest point – 600 m (1962 ft) at the pass through the Beacons beneath Pen y Fan

### Nearest railway

Abergavenny, 19 km (12 miles) southeast of Talybont-on-Usk

### Talybont-on-Usk 1
The Monmouthshire and Brecon Canal cuts through the village, supported by huge retaining walls. It was built between 1797 and 1812 to carry lime, coal and wool 53 km (33 miles) from Brecon to Newport and the Severn Estuary. Lime, from the Trefil quarries south of Talybont, was carried by tramway to the village and shipped in barges. There are remains of a limekiln near the stone bridge south of the river

### Pen y Fan 7
The whole glory of the Brecon Beacons lies spread out below the the 890 m (2907 ft) summit, the highest point in South Wales

### Bwlch (east of the start)
Village set in a gap high in the hills.

###  Refreshments

White Hart PH 🍺, Usk PH, Star PH, tea at the Post Office, **Talybont-on-Usk**
White Hart PH 🍺🍺, **Llanfrynach**

◀ A View from Pen y Fan

Craig Cum Cynwyn

Llanfrynach

600

510

260

220

140

20

25

30   31

60

13

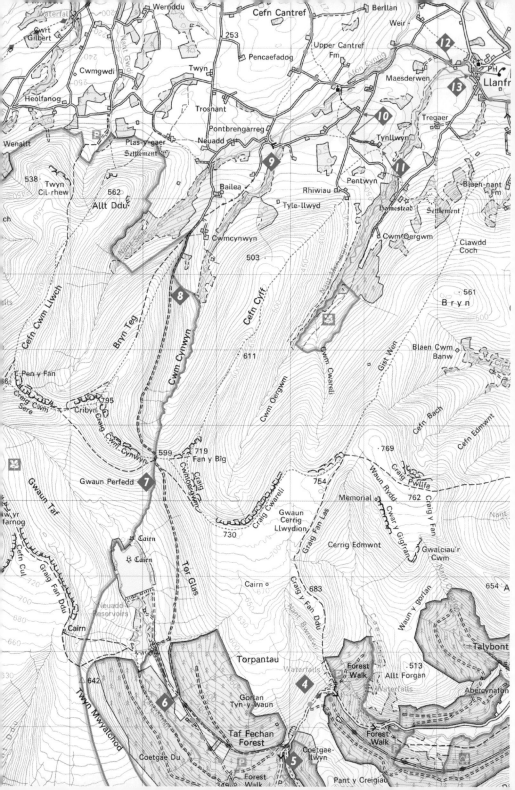

**1** With back to the White Hart PH, L steeply uphill on track. Cross canal. Track swings to the R. Follow blue arrow markers

**2** After 2 km (1¼ miles), at diagonal X-roads with broad, gravel forestry track bear R downhill 'Taff Trail'

**3** Ignore right turn by reservoir dam. Steady 250 m (820 ft) climb for 8 km (5 miles) as views open up

**4** At T-j with road by a cattle grid at the exit of Talybont Forest turn L 'Taff Trail'. Up and over hill

**5 Easy to miss.** On fast descent, immediately after the cattle grid turn R onto track 'Taff Trail. Bridleway', then shortly bear R 'Taff Trail'

**6** At next fork, take lower, LH track through gate 'Taff Trail'. At T-j with road R then immediately R again onto broad stony track 'Unsuitable for motors'. Rough section, muddy in winter

**7** Short, steep drop to cross stream. Steady climb over 3 km (2 miles) to the top of the pass and magnificent views ahead into the Usk Valley

**8** Long, hard, challenging descent on stone track with some rough sections. Track turns to tarmac

**9** Ignore left turn. At T-j R sharply back on yourself to continue downhill. Cross bridge and follow road sharply to the L

**10** After 2 km (1¼ miles) at T-j R uphill 'No entry for MOD Vehicles' then 1st tarmac track L 'Tynllwyn. Bridleway'

*In winter the bridleway may be very muddy. For a road alternative, at T-j L. At next T-j by small triangle of grass R and rejoin at instruction 13*

**11** Follow track past farm leaving barn and farmhouse to the left and turning L at the end of the garden 'Bridleway'. Follow signs along field edge, across field and through gate to cross small stream. Follow the obvious grassy track across fields and through gates

**12** At T-j with road R. At T-j in Llanfrynach turn R 'Taff Trail'

**13** As the road swings L past church turn R onto Victoria Square past telephone box 'Taff Trail'

**14** At T-j with B4558 after 2½ km (1½ miles) R 'Taff Trail'. Follow for 3 km (2 miles) back to the start

# Through forested hills north of Afon Argoed Country Park

This ride explores the forested hills above the river valleys, climbing to a high point of almost 610 m (2000 ft). The route descends into the valley of the Afan River where there are many signs of the area's industrial past, not least the dismantled railway towards the end of the ride, which is followed for several kilometres. As the first half of the ride is one long climb, at times steep, do not be surprised to find that you take up to three quarters of the ride time to get to the high point and that the second half is completed in next to no time.

**Start**

Afan Forest Park & Countryside Centre, Cynonville, 10 km (6 miles) northeast of Port Talbot on the A4107

P Parking: As above

 **Distance and grade**

34 km (21 miles)

Moderate/strenuous

 **Terrain**

River valley, forestry, dismantled railway. One major climb of 510 m (1660 ft) over the first half of the ride with one very steep,

As with all rides in forestry, there is enormous potential for getting lost, so be patient, carry a compass and study the map carefully - new tracks are regularly built making detailed instructions obsolete after a while. Each year there are more waymarked trails through the forests near to the Visitor Centre, so you may wish to explore these as well

Afon Afan

Nant Cregan

190    350    360    470    480

0    5    10    15

short push soon after the start. Lowest point – 91 m (300 ft) at the crossing of River Afan. Highest point – 590 m (1940 ft) near a mast at the highpoint in the forestry

## Nearest railway

Port Talbot, 10 km (6 miles) southwest of the start

◀ *A forest track along the valley of the River Afan*

## Places of interest

### *Afan Argoed Country Park* I
Scenic vale of woods, moorland and streams, Iron Age forts and settlements among hillside farms. Trails start from the Countryside Centre, which houses the Welsh Miners' Museum, with pit gear and simulated coal faces

### *Aberdulais Falls* *(11 km (7 miles) west of the start)*
Turner was one of the many painters and writers drawn to these falls in the late 18th century. The Dulais River tumbles through a gloomy, atmospheric sandstone gorge near its confluence with the River Neath. Remains of old furnaces, weirs and watercourses can also be seen among the thick foliage. As early as 1584, this was a copper works, one of the first industrial sites in South Wales

## Refreshments

*Tea rooms at the start*
*Refreshment Rooms PH,* **Cymer**

Cefn Nant-y-gwair

Mynydd Abergwynfi

Cymer

Duffryn

580

530

490

280

250

180

130

20

25

30

34

*1* From Afan Argoed Centre, cross the A4107, go through bridlegate and bear L. At T-j with steep stone track R downhill. Cross river and follow stone track as it bears L

*2* At T-j at the top of climb turn R sharply back on yourself. After 200 m (yd) leave main track and bear L onto very steep, short push on narrow stone track (blue arrow). At the top, by a blocked up railway tunnel turn sharp L (blue arrow/white bicycle)

*3* The narrow, contouring track joins broader stone track and climbs steeply. At T-j by the ruins of Gyfylchi Chapel with a green metal gate to the left turn R

*4* Follow the main track, ignoring the 1st grassy track to the left. At the next fork bear L on the steeper track

*5* **Ignore** rough tracks to right and left at X-roads, **ignore** left turn and continue climbing. Go over the brow of hill. At the junction of several tracks with fabulous views ahead L uphill

*6* Up and over hill. At X-roads of tracks R uphill (blue arrow/Vale of Neath Walk). After a short climb and short descent take the 1st R uphill

*7* Through (or over) green metal gate and onto track across open moorland. Through (or over) second green metal gate and back into the forest

*8* Cross stream on wide sweeping RH bend, go past derelict mining buildings and follow main track as it turns sharply L uphill. Follow this main track for 4 km (2½ miles) ignoring turnings to right and left

*9* **Easy to miss.** 800 m (½ mile) after spectacular views open up to the left take the first major stone track uphill to the R, opposite a low wooden post with blue arrows. Downhill. **Ignore** right turn as track swings round to the L. Shortly ignore a second right turn as the track starts a long steady climb

*10* 2½ km (1½ miles) after the start of the climb take the 1st stone track to the L which curls uphill through the trees. **Ignore** a left turn

*11* At X-roads at the top with a mast 200 m (yd) to your left turn R downhill towards masts on the horizon (red arrow/Rhondda Community Route). Fine, open descent then undulating track, following red arrows, ignoring several turnings to left and right

*12* **Easy to miss.** After 5½ km (3½ miles) at a large, triangular stone area with a 'quarry' on a slight rise ahead and to the left and a large round metal water barrel at the junction of tracks, turn R. Fast descent

*13* On a RH hairpin bend after 3 km (2 miles) bear L (in effect SA) past a small mast in the woods. Fast descent

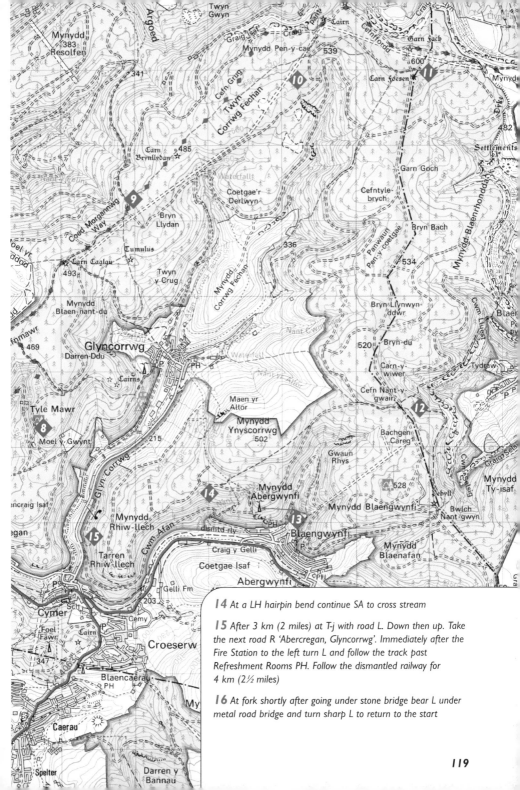

**14** At a LH hairpin bend continue SA to cross stream

**15** After 3 km (2 miles) at T-j with road L. Down then up. Take the next road R 'Abercregan, Glyncorrwg'. Immediately after the Fire Station to the left turn L and follow the track past Refreshment Rooms PH. Follow the dismantled railway for 4 km (2½ miles)

**16** At fork shortly after going under stone bridge bear L under metal road bridge and turn sharp L to return to the start

# 10 Coastline and hills on the Gower Peninsula

**Start**

Oxwich car park, on the coast 16 km (10 miles) southwest of Swansea, to the south of the A4118

P As above (with a charge)

**Distance and grade**

37 km (23 miles)

///// Moderate or strenuous (if you climb to top of Rhossili Down)

**Terrain**

Coastline and heather-clad hills. Two main climbs (and several short climbs) – 190 m (610 ft) from the start to the top of Cefn Bryn; 140 m (460 ft)

Almost an island, the Gower is surrounded by water on three sides, and from the heather- and gorse-clad tops of Cefn Bryn, Llanmadoc Hill and Rhossili Down, which rise to over 180 m (600 ft), there are spectacular views over the whole peninsula. By starting the ride at Oxwich, the worst of the road section comes at the start, including 3 km (2 miles) on the busy A4118. From Penmaen, the ride climbs steeply off-road to the first of the viewpoints with much of the Gower's south coast spread out before you. On fine days, there are views across to Exmoor. The track runs west along the ridge of Cefn Bryn to drop down almost to sea level at Cheriton. A second steep climb along the flanks of Llanmadoc Hill takes you to Llangennith and more opportunities for refreshments. The wide sweep of Rhossili Bay opens up, and at the entrance to the caravan park you have a choice of following the bridleway close to the foot of the hills or of climbing very steeply up onto the top of Rhossili Down for the best views of the whole day. East from here, the route becomes more agricultural in aspect, crossing fields and woodland. A final climb from Scurlage to Hangman's Cross sets you up for a long descent back to Oxwich where, on a hot day, the temptation of the sea may be too much to resist.

from Cheriton up onto Llanmadoc Hill. Optional third very steep climb of 180 m (600 ft) from Hill End to the Beacon on Rhossili Down. Lowest point – sea level at the start. Highest point – 190 m (610 ft) at the top of Cefn Bryn (or 190 m (640 ft) on the hard option above Rhossili Bay)

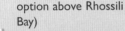

### Nearest railway

Gowerton, 13 km (8 miles) northeast of the route at Penmaen

▼ Rhossili Bay

## Places of interest

### Oxwich Bay 1
Village of stone cottages. The church of St Illtyd on the rocky ledge above the sea dates from the 12th century. Oxwich Castle is a ruined 1541 manor house. There are rare birds and plants at Oxwich Bay, with sand dunes and woodland trails

### Refreshments

Cafes in **Oxwich**
Britannia Inn, **Cheriton**
Kings Head PH, **Llangennith**
Cafes, **Rhossili**
Countryman PH, **Scurlage**

### Llangennith 14
Springs bubble up from the village green surrounded by whitewashed cottages. College Farm stands on the site of a 6th-century monastery founded by St Cenydd. The church lych gate has carved scenes of the saint's life

### Rhossili 16
Colour-washed cottages perch on cliffs above a sandy beach. The church has memorial of Edgar Evans, who died on Scott's 1912 expedition to the South Pole. Rhossili Bay was loved by Dylan Thomas for its wild grandeur

### Gower Farm Museum 20
Old farm buildings house the relics of farming life on the Gower, including household items, agricultural implements and family life memorabilia spanning 100 years

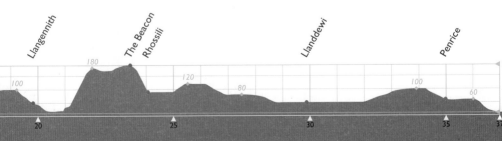

**1** Out of car park turn R towards main road (A4118)

**2** Flat section then steep climb. At T-j with A4118 R 'Swansea'

**3** Follow this busy road for almost 3 km (2 miles) passing church and X-roads in Nicholaston, then 800 m (½ mile) after 'Penmaen'

sign at start of village turn L uphill on road by telephone box and bus shelter

**4** Climb for 600 m (yd) then opposite house on the right with double metal gates turn L steeply uphill onto track. At T-j of tracks L then immediately fork L on the steeper of the two tracks

**5** Climb past stone pumping station of Welsh Water on top of the hill. Fine views open up. Short descent then take LH fork on the hill ahead. Maintain height and bear L

**6** At T-j with road diagonally L onto track, shortly forking R towards trig point. Beyond the trig

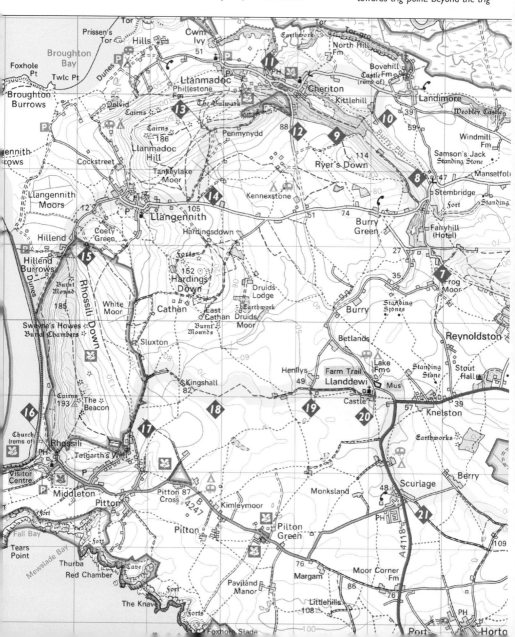

point, there are too many tracks to give instructions for each junction: you are aiming WNW towards the RH set of hills ahead, maintaining height then dropping down to the R

**7** At T-j with broad stone track (with any luck, somewhere near Little End Farm) bear L. Track becomes tarmac. At X-roads (white lines across road) turn R 'Fairyhill'

**8** At T-j on sharp bend L 'Llangennith' then after 150 m (yd) uphill 1st track R 'Bridleway'. **Take care** – this is a turn on a blind bend – cross the road either before or after the junction, where it is safer

**9** Follow stone track to its end. At farmhouse SA onto grassy track. Enter woodland and bear R steeply downhill on stone track. Cross stream and climb steeply

**10** At T-j with gravel track by barn conversion L. At T-j with road L

**11** At T-j by Britannia Inn L 'Llangennith'

**12** Climb steeply for 800 m (½ mile). Shortly after the second house on the left, turn sharp R steeply uphill on broad gravel track

**13** Follow the stone track to its end by the second house and go SA onto enclosed, grassy track. At a ruined house turn L downhill on grass track, taking RH fork to join better stone track

**14** At T-j with road R. Go past pub and church in Llangennith. At small roundabout at the end of the village L 'Hillend'

**15** Immediately before the entrance to the caravan site turn L through bridlegate 'NT Rhossili Down'. Fork R for low-level route beneath the hillside with fine sea

views (**Or** fork L for very steep push to the top of hill with magnificent views of all the Gower

**16** The two options merge. At T-j with road L (**Or** turn R for cafes in Rhossili). After 800 m (½ mile) 1st L by bus shelter and telephone box onto no through road

**17** At the end of tarmac fork R. After 1 km (¾ mile), go through gate and follow track round RH bend ('Private' sign on track ahead). Shortly, fork R onto stone track

**18** Pass ruin, along RH edge of 1st field, LH edge of second field then through gate onto enclosed track. At exit bear L diagonally across field and through gate onto second enclosed section

**19** Pass farm. At fork R through gate onto grassy track

**20** At T-j with road by Gower Farm Museum R. At T-j with A4118 R 'Port Eynon'

**21** After 2 km (1¼ miles) 1st road L 'Berry'. At T-j by farm R. Tarmac turns to track

**22** Track narrows then swings R by ruined house. At T-j with road L for 1 km (¾ mile) then 1st road R by triangle of grass 'Oxwich'

**23** Follow road round LH hairpin bend 'Oxwich'. At X-roads L then R to return to the car park at the start

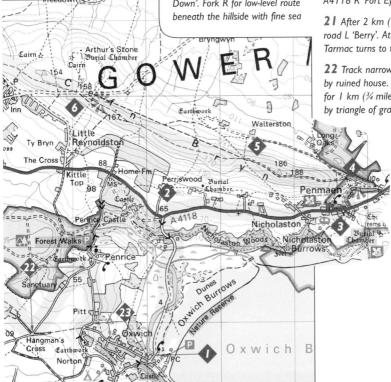

*Notes*

*Notes*

*Notes*

*Notes*

# Useful addresses

**British Cycling Federation**
National Cycling Centre
Stuart Street
Manchester M11 4DQ
0870 871 2000
www.bcf.uk.com

The BCF co-ordinates and promotes an array of cycle sports and cycling in general. They are a good first point of contact if you want to find out more about how to get involved in cycling. The website provides information on upcoming cycle events and competitions.

**CTC (Cyclists Touring Club)**
Cotterell House
69 Meadrow
Godalming
Surrey GU7 3HS
01483 417217
www.ctc.org.uk

Britain's largest cycling organisation, promoting recreational and utility cycling. The CTC provides touring and technical advice, legal aid and insurance, and campaigns to improve facilities and opportunities for all cyclists. The website provides details of campaigns and routes and has an online application form.

**The London Cycling Campaign**
Unit 228
30 Great Guildford Street
London SE1 0HS
020 7928 7220
www.lcc.org.uk

The LCC promotes cycling in London by providing services for cyclists and by campaigning for more facilities for cyclists. Membership of the LCC provides the following benefits: London Cyclist magazine, insurance, legal advice, workshops, organised rides, discounts in bike shops and much more. You can join the LCC on its website.

**Sustrans**
Head Office
Crown House
37-41 Prince Street
Bristol BS1 4PS
General information line: 0117 929 0888
www.sustrans.org.uk

A registered charity, Sustrans designs and builds systems for sustainable transport. It is best known for its transformation of old railway lines into safe, traffic-free routes for cyclists and pedestrians and wheelchair users. Sustrans is developing the 13,000 km (8000 mile) National Cycle Network on traffic-calmed minor roads and traffic-free paths, to be completed by the year 2005 with major funding from the Millennium Commission.

**Veteran Cycle Club**
Membership Secretary
31 Yorke Road
Croxley Green
Rickmansworth
Herts WD3 3DW
www.v-cc.org.uk

A very active club, the VCC is concerned with the history and restoration of veteran cycles. Members enjoy organised rides and receive excellent publications relating to cycle history and club news.